THE ROCK TOMBS OF EL~HAWAWISH

THE CEMETERY OF AKHMIM

by

Naguib Kanawati

VOLUME IV

Published by The Macquarie Ancient History Association
with the support of The Rundle Foundation for Egyptian Archaeology

To the memory of
A. Abu-Bakr

ISBN: 0-908299-06-0

Published by: The Macquarie Ancient History Association
with the support of: The Rundle Foundation for Egyptian Archaeology
Macquarie University, Sydney, N.S.W. 2113, Australia

Printed by Adept Printing Co.
14 Clements Avenue, Bankstown, N.S.W. 2200, Australia

Distributed by: Aris and Phillips Ltd.
Church Street, Warminster, Wilts, England.

The excavation at El-Hawawish is a project of
the Ancient History Documentary Research Centre of Macquarie University

PREFACE

The major focus of the excavations this season – December 1982-January 1983 – was upon square M, in a section believed to be extensively used at the end of Dynasty 5 and the beginning of Dynasty 6. Work on the tomb of Hesi-Min, M22, which began in the previous season, was completed, together with three undecorated tombs, M27-M29, which appear to form a single group with M22. A limited amount of excavations was also conducted in square H where tomb H14 was cleared and recorded, mainly for its architectural features. Clearance began in the latter part of the season in tombs M21 and M23, and the smaller ancilliary tombs surrounding them, all believed to be from the Fifth Dynasty. Work on these will continue in the next season. Considerable progress was made in the survey of the mountain, with possibly one-half of the tombs now numbered and located on the map. Special attention was given to preservation of the wall scenes in tombs excavated in previous seasons. The complete results of the survey and preservation will be included among other studies of the site in a special volume which will also contain an index to all previous volumes.

The project which started last year of publishing the coffins from Akhmim, which for the most part are now in the Cairo Museum, has continued with two more coffins included in the present volume. It was also decided to publish any inscribed fragments known to have come from Akhmim with the hope of compiling all information relating to this province during the period under consideration. Although most of these coffins and fragments have appeared in previous publications (Lacau, *Sarcophages*, and Borchardt, *Denkmäler*), their inclusion in the present work aims at providing detailed facsimiles and photographs for the study of artistic and palaeographical details.

In the measurement of the finds, the following abbreviations are used: H. = height; D. = diameter; BW. = body width; Th. = thickness. In numbering the finds, H refers to El-Hawawish, followed by the year the object was found. The second letter refers to the square in which the tomb is located according to the present survey, followed by the tomb number. The last figure is the number given to the item in consecutive order.

Financial support has been received this season from the Australian Research Grants Scheme, the National Geographic Society, The Macquarie University Research Grants, the Australian Institute of Archaeology, the Macquarie Ancient History Association and the Rundle Foundation for Egyptian Archaeology. The generosity of these sponsors have made the project possible.

I was fortunate to have the assistance of a capable and enthusiastic team. My research assistant, Mrs. Ann McFarlane, gave a great deal of help on the site and in the preparation of this volume. Mr. Naguib Maksoud (Alexandria) produced the numerous intricate architectural drawings printed here. Mr. Nabil Charoubim (Cairo Museum) was responsible for the fine work of inking all the scenes. Miss Joan Beck (Macquarie University) took charge of recording and drawing the pottery finds. Mr. John Curro (University of New South Wales) undertook the surveying of a large section of the mountain and his work will appear in a later volume. Mr. Adel Abdel-Aziz (University of Alexandria) again supervised the field work. The photography this season was done by Miss Laura Baker (Meadowbank Technical College) and Mr. Mustafa Abdel-Maqsud and Mr. Kamal Mustafa (Cairo Museum). Miss Maureen Buzacott and Miss Mara Franco (Macquarie University) assisted with the cleaning, tracing and preservation of wall scenes. To them all, I extend my sincere appreciation.

The Egyptian Antiquities Organisation was always willing to provide any help to facilitate our task. In particular, I would like to thank the Chairman, Dr. Ahmed Kadri; the Director of the Museums Sector, Dr. Dia' Abou-Ghazi; the Director of the Cairo Museum, Dr. Mohamed Saleh, and his most helpful staff. My thanks are also extended to Dr. Ali El-Khouli and Mr. Metawé Balboush. The co-operation of Mr. Rifaat A. Farag, Mr. Yehya Salah El-Masry and Mr. Mohsen L. Riyad of the Inspectorate of Antiquities at Sohag is particularly appreciated.

The final art work for this volume was prepared by the Audio-Visual Services Unit of Macquarie University, and I would like to acknowledge the contribution of Mr. Tan Teong Eng from the Art Section, and of Messrs. John Papadopoulos, Reece Scannell and Joe Vissel from the Photography Section.

Mr. T. G. H. James (British Museum) and Mr. Greg Horsley (Macquarie University) were kind enough to read the original manuscript and to suggest many improvements, for which I am particularly grateful. Similarly, I am most appreciative of helpful comments received from Dr. H. G. Fischer and Dr. K. A. Kitchen.

I wish also to acknowledge the support and encouragement that this project receives from my colleagues at Macquarie University, in particular Assoc. Professor Bruce Harris, Professor Edwin Judge and Assoc. Professor Raoul Mortley. Similarly, my appreciation goes to the Rundle Foundation for Egyptian Archaeology and Macquarie Ancient History Association, which together make possible the publication of this volume.

Naguib Kanawati

ABBREVIATIONS

ASAE: *Annales du Service des Antiquités de l'Égypte.*
Badawy, *Iteti:* Badawy, Alexander, *The Tombs of Iteti, Sekhem-ʿankh-Ptah, and Kaemnofert at Giza* (Berkeley, 1976).
Baer, *Rank and Title:* Baer, Klaus, *Rank and Title in the Old Kingdom: The Structure of the Egyptian Administration in the Fifth and Sixth Dynasties* (Chicago, 1960).
Barta, *Opferliste:* Barta, Winfried, *Die altägyptische Opferliste von der Frühzeit bis zur griechisch-römischen Epoche* (Berlin, 1963).
Blackman, *Meir:* Blackman, Aylward M., *The Rock Tombs of Meir,* 6 vols. (London, 1914-53).
Borchardt, *Denkmäler:* Borchardt, Ludwig, *Denkmäler des Alten Reiches* (Catalogue général du Musée du Caire), 2 vols. (Cairo, 1937, 1964).
Brunner, *Felsgräber:* Brunner, Hellmut, *Die Anlagen der ägyptischen Felsgräber bis zum Mittleren Reich* (Glückstadt, 1936).
Brunner-Traut, *Seschemnofers III:* Brunner-Traut, Emma, *Die altägyptische Grabkammer Seschemnofers III aus Gîsa* (Mainz am Rhein, 1977).
CRIPEL: *Cahier de Recherches de l'Institut de Papyrologie et de'Egyptologie de Lille: Études sur l'Egypte et le Soudan anciens.*
Davies, *Ptahhetep:* Davies, Norman de G., *The Mastaba of Ptahhetep and Akhethetep at Saqqarah,* 2 vols. (London, 1900-1901).
Davies, *Sheikh Saïd:* Davies, Norman de G., *The Rock Tombs of Sheikh Saïd* (London, 1901).
Davies, *Deir el-Gebrâwi:* Davies, Norman de G., *The Rock Tombs of Deir el-Gebrâwi,* 2 vols. (London, 1902).
Drenkhahn, *Handwerker:* Drenkhahn, Rosemarie, *Die Handwerker und ihre Tatigkeiten im Alten Ägypten* (Wiesbaden, 1976).
Duell, *Mereruka:* Duell, Prentice, *The Mastaba of Mereruka,* 2 vols. (Chicago, 1938).
Dunham-Simpson, *Mersyankh III:* Dunham, D. and Simpson, W.K., *The Mastaba of Queen Mersyankh III:* G 7530-7540 (Boston, 1974).
Edel, *Grammatik:* Edel, Elmar, *Altägyptische Grammatik,* 2 vols. (Rome, 1955, 1964).
Epron-Wild, *Ti:* Epron, L.–Wild, H., *Le tombeau de Ti, MIFAO* 65, 3 fascs. (Cairo, 1939-66).
Erman, *Reden:* Erman, Adolf, *Reden, Rufe und Lieder auf Gräberbildern des Alten Reiches,* APAW (Berlin, 1919).
Fischer, *Dendera:* Fischer, Henry G., *Dendera in the Third Millennium B.C. Down to the Theban Domination of Upper Egypt* (New York, 1968).
Fischer, *Varia:* Fischer, Henry G., *Egyptian Studies I: Varia* (New York, 1976).
Fischer, *Calligraphy:* Fischer, Henry G., *Ancient Egyptian Calligraphy* (New York, 1979).
Gamer-Wallert, *Fische:* Gamer-Wallert, I., *Fische und Fischkulte im alten Ägypten* (Wiesbaden, 1970).
Gomaà, *Ersten Zwischenzeit:* Gomaà, Farouk, *Ägypten während der Ersten Zwischenzeit* (Wiesbaden, 1980).
Hassan, *Giza:* Hassan, Selim, *Excavations at Giza,* 10 vols. (Oxford/Cairo, 1929-60).
El-Hawawish: Kanawati, Naguib, *The Rock Tombs of El-Hawawish: The Cemetery of Akhmim,* 3 vols. (Sydney, 1980-82).
James, *Hieroglyphic Texts:* James, T.G.H., *Hieroglyphic Texts from Egyptian Stelae etc., British Museum,* I (London, 1961).
Junker, *Gîza:* Junker, Hermann, *Gîza,* 12 vols. (Vienna, 1929-55).
Kanawati, *Governmental Reforms:* Kanawati, Naguib, *Governmental Reforms in Old Kingdom Egypt* (Warminster, 1980).
LAAA: *Annals of Archaeology and Anthropology, Liverpool.*
Lacau, *Sarcophages:* Lacau, P., *Sarcophages antérieurs au Nouvel Empire* (Catalogue général du Musée du Caire) 2 vols. (Cairo, 1904-1906).
Lepsius, *Denkmäler:* Lepsius, C.R., *Denkmäler aus Ägypten und Äthiopien,* 12 vols. (Berlin, 1849-59): *Text,* 5 vols., and *Ergänzungsband* (Leipzig, 1897-1913).
Mackay, *Hemamieh:* Mackay, E.–Harding, L.–Petrie, W.M.F., *Bahrein and Hemamieh* (London, 1929).
Mariette, *Mastabas:* Mariette, Auguste, *Les mastabas de l'Ancien Empire* (Paris, 1889).
Martin-Pardey, *Provinzialverwaltung:* Martin-Pardey, Eva, *Untersuchungen zur ägyptischen Provinzialverwaltung bis zum Ende des Alten Reiches* (Hildesheim, 1976).
MMJ: *The Metropolitan Museum Journal.*
Mohr, *Hetep-her-akhti:* Mohr, Herta T., *The Mastaba of Hetep-her-akhti* (Leiden, 1943).
Montet, *Vie privée:* Montet, P., *Les scènes de la vie privée dans les tombeaux égyptiens de l'Ancien Empire* (Strasbourg, 1925).
de Morgan, *Dahchour,* Morgan, J. de, *Fouilles à Dahchour,* 2 vols. (Vienna, 1895, 1903).
Moussa-Altenmüller, *Nefer:* Moussa, Ahmed-Altenmüller, Hartwig, *The Tomb of Nefer and Ka-Hay* (Mainz am Rhein, 1971).
Moussa-Junge, *Two Tombs:* Moussa, Ahmed-Junge, Friedrich, *Two Tombs of Craftsmen* (Mainz/Rhein, 1975).
Moussa-Altenmüller, *Nianchchnum:* Moussa, Ahmed-Altenmüller, Hartwig, *Das Grab des Nianchchnum und Chnumhotep* (Mainz/Rhein, 1977).
Petrie, *Deshasheh:* Petrie, William M.F., *Deshasheh* (London, 1898).
Petrie, *Athribis:* Petrie, William M.F., *Athribis* (London, 1908).
Petrie-Murray, *Tomb Chapels:* Petrie, Hilda–Murray, Margaret A., *Seven Memphite Tomb Chapels* (London, 1952).
Rachewiltz, *Irw-K3-Ptḥ:* Rachewiltz, Boris de, *The Rock Tomb of Irw-K3-Ptḥ* (Leiden, 1960).
Ranke, *Personennamen:* Ranke, Hermann, *Die altägyptischen Personennamen,* 3 vols. (Glückstadt, 1935-77).
Reisner, *Giza:* Reisner, George A., *A History of the Giza Necropolis* 1 (Cambridge, Mass., 1942); Reisner, G.A.–Smith, W.S., *A History of the Giza Necropolis* 2 (Cambridge, Mass., 1955).
SAK: *Studien zur Altägyptischen Kultur.*
Saleh, *Tombs at Thebes:* Saleh, Mohamed, *Three Old-Kingdom Tombs at Thebes* (Mainz am Rhein, 1977).
Schäfer, *Principles:* Schäfer, Heinrich, *Principles of Egyptian Art.* Translated by John Baines (Oxford, 1974).
Simpson, *Kawab:* Simpson, William K., *The Mastabas of Kawab, Khafkhufu I and II* (Boston, 1978).
Simpson, *Western Cemetery:* Simpson, William K., *Mastabas of the Western Cemetery:* Part I (Boston, 1980).
Smith, *HESPOK:* Smith, William Stevenson, *A History of Egyptian Sculpture and Painting in the Old Kingdom* (London, 1946).
Vandier, *Manuel:* Vandier, Jacques, *Manuel d'archéologie égyptienne,* 6 vols. (Paris, 1952-78).
Varille, *Ni-ankh-Pepi:* Varille, Alexandre, *La tombe de Ni-ankh-Pepi a Zaouyet El-Mayetîn* (Cairo, 1938).
Wiebach, *Scheintür:* Wiebach, Silvia, *Die Ägyptische Scheintür* (Hamburg, 1981).
ZÄS: *Zeitschrift für ägyptische Sprache und Altertumskunde.*

CONTENTS

PLATES

FIGURES

THE TOMB OF HESI-MIN

M 22*

I THE TOMB OWNER, HIS FAMILY AND DEPENDANTS

The Tomb Owner

NAME

Ḥzjj-Mnw 'Hesi-Min'. This name, which is not listed in Ranke, *Personennamen,* may mean 'a favoured of Min'. The *z* is placed before *ḥz* probably for graphic reasons. However, it may be argued that the *z* should be taken separately, and not as a phonetic complement, in which case the name should be read as *Z-ḥzjj-Mnw* 'a man favoured of Min'.

TITLES

1 – *jmj-r z3w Šmꜥ* 'overseer of the phyles of Upper Egypt'.[1]
2 – *jmj-r k3t nt nswt* 'overseer of the works of the king'.
3 – *wr mḏ Šmꜥ* 'greatest of the ten of Upper Egypt'.[2]
4 – *rḫ nswt* 'acquaintance of the king'.[3]
5 – *ḥm-nṯr Mnw* 'priest of Min'.
6 – s [. . .] – *nswt* '. . . of the king'.

THE RANKING OF HESI-MIN'S TITLES

The following chart is based on the strings of titles recorded on the false door:

wr mḏ Šmꜥ
|
jmj-r k3t nt nswt
|
jmj-r z3w Šmꜥ — *rḫ nswt*
|
ḥm-nṯr Mnw

The order is different on the north wall of the shrine:

rḫ nswt
|
wr mḏ Šmꜥ

The Wife of Hesi-Min

NAME(S)

Špsjt-k3w.[4] The name has survived in full only on the southern false door, where its bearer is not referred to as 'his wife'. But this relationship may be understood from some traces of inscriptions above [*Špsjt*]*-k3w,* where she accompanies the tomb owner in his fishing boat, on the west wall of the chapel. If *Špsjt-k3w* was the same as the owner of an unfinished stela from Akhmim and now in the Cairo Museum[5] (see description below), then she also bore the 'beautiful name' *Jrjt.*[6] Yet the stela appears to be of a later date than the tomb under consideration. From the fragmentary inscriptions above the wife shown on both thicknesses of the doorway her name may be reconstructed as *Ḥknw-Mwt* (not listed by Ranke, *Personennamen*). Whether this was a second name of *Špsjt-k3w* or that of a different wife is uncertain.

TITLES

1 – *rḫ(t) nswt* 'acquaintance of the king'.
2 – *ḥm(t)-nṯr Nt* 'priestess of Neith'.
3 – *ḥm(t)-nṯr Ḥwt-ḥr nb(t) nht* 'priestess of Hathor lady of the sycamore'.
4 – *ḥm(t)-nṯr Ḥqt(?)* 'priestess of Heket(?)'. The title is recorded by Newberry,[7] but no trace of it is now found in the tomb.

The Sons of Hesi-Min

1 – *Nj-ꜥnḫ-Mnw.* Ranke translates as 'Besitzer von Leben ist Min'.[8] He is represented in front of his father in the spear fishing scene on the west wall of the chapel, with the designation *z3.f smsw* 'his eldest son', and the title *ḥm-nṯr Mnw* 'priest of Min'. He is probably the same

son as the one shown before Hesi-Min on the north wall of the shrine.

2 – *Nb-ʿnḫ-Mnw*. Ranke translates as 'ein Herr des Lebens ist Min'.[9] He appears on the false door, designated as *z3.f* 'his son'.

3 – *Nṯrj-rn-Mnw*. According to Ranke the name means 'göttlich ist der Name des Min'.[10] He is shown on the above mentioned false door and on the west wall of the chapel, described as *z3.f* 'his son'.

4 – *Nfr-s*[. . .?]*-Mnw*. The area immediately to the left of the *s* is damaged, and may have contained one or two more signs, i.e., *sfḫ*, *sšm*, or the like. He also appears on the west wall of the chapel.

5 – A man shown behind the son *Nṯrj-rn-Mnw* in the family fishing scene is labelled as . . . *f* . . ., and may have been a son of Hesi-Min, perhaps *Nb-ʿnḫ-Mnw*, as these two sons are also depicted together on the false door.

Dependants of Hesi-Min

1 – *ʿnḫw*.[11] He appears on the left outer jamb of the false door.
ḥm-k3 'ka-servant'.

2 – *Q3j-Mnw*.[12] He is represented in the bottom register on the south wall and in the second lower one on the west wall of the chapel.
jmj-r ṯzt 'master drover'.

Titles of Unnamed Dependants

On the west wall of the chapel:
jmj-r pr 'steward'.
zš 'scribe' (two individuals).

On the north wall of the shrine:
ḥm-k3 'ka-servant'.

II DATING OF HESI-MIN

There is no conclusive evidence for the dating of this official, but the following points together may help us assign him to a reasonably secure date.

1 – M22 and some others of the largest tombs in the cemetery are cut into the southern face of the mountain. Study of the conditions there suggests that this was the most appropriate, and hence probably the earliest, section of the mountain to be chosen by tomb owners. The area has advantages geographically, being in a semi-circular bend, which seems to have some climatic benefits, in addition to offering an imposing view of the Nile. The rock formation here is visibly better than anywhere else on the mountain, being of compact limestone (as against the conglomerate limestone in other parts of the mountain), which enabled artists to obtain hard, smooth surfaces suitable for reliefs and statues cut in the living rock, as well as for painted decoration.

2 – Situated at the height of 190m. above the mean sea level, M22 is one of the lowest major tombs on the mountain. As the cutting of these main tombs appears to have progressed from the lower level upwards,[13] a relatively early date is likely for M22.

3 – Chapels with long north-south corridors are characteristic of the Fifth and the Sixth Dynasties. This appears to be the case at Giza[14] and Saqqara.[15] In the provinces, however, this type is very rare, and a comparison with the tombs at Hemamia (end of Dynasty 5) is useful.[16]

4 – There appears to be a tendency at El-Hawawish during the Sixth Dynasty, to change from the vertical shafts, common in the earlier tombs, to the sloping passages leading to burial chambers.[17] Vertical shafts are regularly used in M22, and it is interesting that even after the cutting of a sloping passage (II) and a burial chamber for the tomb owner, a vertical shaft was then excavated into the floor of this chamber leading to a second, complete burial chamber in which Hesi-Min was buried.

5 – Accompanying the change in the type of shafts, a change in the composition of the wall plaster seems to have taken place. In the earlier tombs, including M22, a white gypsum plaster was used, but this was replaced in later tombs of the middle of Dynasty 6 by the light brown plaster which became common in this cemetery.[18]

6 – Like the late Fifth Dynasty tombs at Hemamia,[19] Sheikh Said,[20] and Saqqara,[21] M22 makes use of rock-cut statues.[22]

7 – A brief study of the scenes and inscriptions in M22 shows that they have close affinities with others dating from the latter part of Dynasty 5. The scenes in M22 are lively and full of grace, yet crowded with details, particularly with regard to offerings on the south wall of the chapel.[23] The colouring is very attractive. The tomb owner is shown twice (on the south wall and on the false door) seated on a chair with bulls' legs, a style which was gradually being supplanted by lions' legs.[24] Chairs with bulls' legs appear to be more in use until the end of Dynasty 5,[25] and the evidence from El-Hawawish suggests a consistent change to the lions' legs after the end of this dynasty. On the false door the wife holds the lotus flower from the upper part of the stem, in the typical Old Kingdom manner;[26] and the theme of presenting lotus flowers to the tomb owner, as on the south wall, appears to be more common in the Fifth Dynasty, particularly in its latter part.[27] On the same wall the soundbox of the harp is decorated with the *wḏ3t*-eye, as is the case in the tomb of Ni-ankh-Khenum at Saqqara,[28] dated to the reign of Menkauhor by Moussa and Altenmuller.[29] The spear fishing scene also contains features similar to those found in the tomb of Ni-ankh-Khenum. Whereas the spear is usually held almost horizontally (at an angle of approximately 10°) in Old Kingdom tombs, it is held at an angle of 22° by Hesi-Min and of 30° by Ni-ankh-Khenum.[30] The representation of the tomb owner's wife standing next to him in the fishing boat, and clasping his leg, was familiar during the latter part of the Fifth Dynasty.[31]

On the south wall of the chapel in M22 is a small section of what was almost certainly a desert hunting scene, formed of two (?) superposed wavy lines with animals on them (see below). The earliest examples of such a composition in private tombs are to be found in the mastabas of Ptah-hetep and Seshem-nefer,[32] both from the end of the Fifth Dynasty. The representation of spear fishing in private tombs occurred also for the first time at this same period.[33] Although not restricted to one period, the frieze in the form 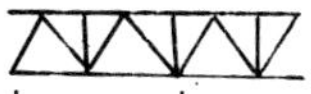 above the scenes appears to have been common at the end of Dynasty 5.[34] Not many inscriptions have survived in M22, yet the writing of the *w3* sign without the forked tail (in *rn jw3*, on the south wall), is indicative of an earlier date than that of the Sixth Dynasty tombs at El-Hawawish.[35] The similarity between the writing of the *m* on our false door and in the mastabas of Ptah-hetep[36] and Ti[37] is also evident.

8 – The false door is of the simple type (II 2), which, according to Rusch appeared under Menkaure, became dominant in the Fifth Dynasty, particularly in its first half, and continued in Dynasty 6.[38] The shape of the false door should, however, be used only as an indication for a broad date, and should be considered with other evidence.[39]

9 – Based on the presence of the title *rḫ nswt* 'acquaintance of the king' among Hesi-Min's titulary, as recorded by Newberry,[40] and the assumption that this title was not held by provincial officials after the Fifth Dynasty, Fischer dates the tomb under consideration to Dynasty 5.[41] This date is followed by Gomaà, who also raises the possibility of identifying Hesi-Min's eldest son, Ni-ankh-Min, with the similarly named owner of tomb number 23 of Newberry,[42] whom Gomaà places at the beginning of Dynasty 6.[43] This relationship seems likely, yet one should bear in mind the following points: (a) that the name is written as *N-ʿnḫ-Mnw* in our tomb, but *ʿnḫ-Mnw* or *Mnw-ʿnḫ* in tomb number 23. These could of course be variants of the same name; (b) that

the eldest son of Hem-Min, owner of the neighbouring tomb, M43 (to be published),[44] is also named Min-ankh. However, support for Gomaà's suggestion may now be found in the fact that like the owner of tomb number 23, Hesi-Min held the title *jmj-r z3w Šmᶜ* 'overseer of the phyles of Upper Egypt', and it is possible that *Mnw-ᶜnḫ* may have succeeded his father in this office.[45] The title is not held by any other official found in this cemetery.

10 – Two ranking systems were used in listing Hesi-Min's titles. (a) On the false door: *wr mḏ Šmᶜ, jmj-r k3t nt nswt, rḫ nswt.* (b) On the north wall of the shrine: *rḫ nswt, wr mḏ Šmᶜ*. It is reasonable to think that the false door would be the first part of the tomb to receive decoration, and that the difference in the order of titles on the north wall was the result of their being inscribed at a slightly later time, when the ranking system had changed. The two periods, according to Baer's study, which accommodate such a change are VB (Neferirkare to Djedkare) for inscription (a), and VC (Djedkare to Unis) for inscription (b).[46] Thus the reign of Djedkare is the most likely for the decoration of the chapel.

11 – At this stage a comparison with Ka-khent (the father)[47] of Hemamia is particularly useful. Some similarities in art and architecture of M22 and the tomb of Ka-khent have been mentioned above. In addition, the wives of the two men held similar titles: 'acquaintance of the king, priestess of Hathor' and 'priestess of Neith'.[48] The last title, which is uncommon among provincial women, may indicate an origin from the capital. Both men had also the same titles: 'greatest of the ten of Upper Egypt, overseer of the phyles of Upper Egypt', and 'acquaintance of the king'.[49] But unlike all provincial officials known from the Old Kingdom they share the responsibility of 'overseer of the works of the king',[50] although in the case of Ka-khent it is sometimes restricted to 'the middle provinces of Upper Egypt'.[51] Considering the state of preservation in M22, one cannot be certain whether the same restriction of office applies also there, although this seems unlikely. It appears to me that the two men were contemporaries, and that they were part of a governmental reform late in Dynasty 5, probably under Djedkare, when Upper Egypt was administered for the first time by officials residing there and not in the capital where their career might have begun.[52]

Suggested date: late Dynasty 5, probably under Djedkare.

III ARCHITECTURAL FEATURES

Figs. 1 – 4.

This large tomb is one of a group dating to the late Fifth Dynasty, probably the earliest period to have been excavated at El-Hawawish. As such its position is well chosen at a height of 190 metres above mean sea level, approximately 6.00m. below that of Tjeti/Kai-hep (M8).[53] Lying in a protected semi-circular bend of the southern face of the mountain, it has an imposing view of the Nile. Here, also, the quality of rock is exceptionally good, perhaps the best in the mountain, and provides smooth, hard surfaces for painted decoration, for sculptured relief on entrances, and for statues cut in the mother rock within the chapels. The scale and style of the architecture and its decorative details are a result of both the texture and structural properties of this rock.

The Forecourt

The façade of this tomb is hewn deeply into the mountainside, resulting in an impressive approach. A long, but narrow, forecourt area, with smoothly cut and well preserved surfaces, slopes upward at a 5° angle in a northerly direction to the entrance. It measures 9.75m. N-S (from the façade to the south wall of Pit i) and 4.25m. E-W (from the fence to the east wall). This forecourt is unusually narrow for such a large tomb and probably was not extended further westward because of the excavation at a lower level of a large forecourt belonging to the adjacent and earlier tomb M23. To provide protection from a dangerous drop of over 3.00m. into the forecourt of M23, a low, broad, horizontal fence was left in the mother rock on the western side of the forecourt of M22. It runs the full length of the forecourt, giving it a terraced appearance. This low fence measures 2.55m. wide and approximately .50m. high at the northern end and 1.20m. high at the southern end.

The full length of the eastern side of the forecourt is defined by a wall cut into the slope of the mountain. This wall is now irregular in height, being broken at the northern end and possibly at the top as well. At the highest remaining point it reaches 2.30m. Into this wall open three small tombs (M27, M28, M29; see below). Their entrances are well executed but, viewed from the forecourt, there is nothing to distinguish the width of their individual façades, so that this wall has a smooth and continuous line. Nine vertical shafts are located in the forecourt, five of which (Pits e – i) are contiguous with the east wall. The mouths of all of these shafts are cut on the same sloping line as the floor of the forecourt, rather than on the horizontal, and most of them are square in shape.

The sloping façade measures 6.85m. wide (assuming that it extends to the western edge of the low fence) and has an average height of 3.60m., but is broken and uneven in many parts. From the top it slopes slightly out to a base line .20m. from the perpendicular line of the doorway. The eastern side of the façade is cut at a right angle to the entrance. Further eastward, the wall originally separating M22 from M27 is preserved only to a height of 1.25m., being almost entirely broken away in its upper part. The western side is cut at a slight angle to the doorway, the section over the low fence appearing to be separated from that adjacent to the doorway by a shoulder or protrusion left in the rock.

In the façade on the western side a niche is cut at a height of 1.00m. above the low fence. Although the opening in the façade is chipped, the internal surfaces are smooth, and the measurements of the niche can be reconstructed as .70m. deep x 1.00m wide x 1.10m. high. This niche is almost the same size as one cut in the façade of the adjacent tomb M23 at a height of about 4.00m. At this height its purpose is unlikely to have been to receive offerings, and it is possible that both niches may have accommodated small statues. At the sill height of the niche of M22 and in front of it on the left side is a rather irregular projection in the rock measuring approximately 1.00m. x 1.20m. The purpose of this is not clear.

The Chapel

Access to the chapel is through a doorway, well cut but now quite broken, which measures 1.20m. thick x .90m. wide x 2.40m. high from below the drum. The portion of a drum which remains is .50m. high, but there is no sign of an external lintel. Both door thicknesses were decorated with reliefs, now badly damaged and weathered. Two steps, one .10m. high and the second .20m. high, lead to the floor of the chapel. The interior of the doorway is defined by an internal door recess .35m. deep x 1.20m. wide x 2.90m. high.

The entrance, in the central part of the south wall, leads to a chapel, exceptionally well cut with sharp right angles. Into the north wall of the chapel is cut a long shrine. (The terms 'chapel' and 'shrine' are used here simply to distinguish the two areas from each other, the shrine being the room or recess in which the tomb owner's false door is placed.) Both floor and ceiling are perfectly parallel throughout, and on the same level. The nature of the rock in this area enabled the builder to have smooth surfaces, as well as statues cut in the mother rock. For this same reason the tomb has suffered more than any other on the mountain. As a source of good quality stone, all the walls have been quarried into with the exception of the southwest corner which retains a large portion of its scenes. In many cases small sections were left, perhaps to support the ceiling, which probably misled Newberry to believe it to be a pillared hall.[54] There is no evidence that the roof was ever supported by pillars. As well as the damage done by quarrying, the south wall to the east of the doorway is so badly broken that very little remains above a height of 1.25m. Fortunately, from both ceiling and floor levels the remaining outlines provide exact measurements.

It appears that all surfaces in the chapel were covered with a fine white gypsum plaster and decorated with painting. Even the walls which are largely quarried away have traces of colour still visible just below the ceiling. Fragments of painted plaster indicate that the internal door recess was probably painted in red with black spots (in imitation of red granite (?), or just as a decorative motif), as were the walls below the scenes to a height of 1.00m., a narrow band between the ceiling and the top of the decorative frieze, the jambs and niche of the southern false door and the drum of the northern false door, and the ceiling of the shrine area. The ceiling of the chapel itself shows no trace of colour and possibly was never painted. The thicknesses and the inner walls of the statue niches, as well as the statues themselves, are plastered and painted in a creamy colour wash, and where the background has survived, decorative, scattered red spots appear.

The shorter E-W section of the tomb forms the chapel area which measures 9.10m. E-W x 3.05m. N-S x 3.75m. high. As mentioned above, virtually nothing survives of the upper part of the south wall to the east of the doorway. However, the same wall to the west of the entrance and the west wall retain a major portion of clear and colourful scenes and inscriptions which are in a reasonably good state of preservation.

Most of the north wall has been largely quarried away, but in the lower part of the western half, cut into the mother rock, is a statue niche for two figures, presumably the tomb owner and his wife. It is symmetrical with two jambs of equal measurements and was probably plastered and painted as remaining fragments of plaster attest. Due to the quarrying it is impossible to determine the original height. The sill of the niche is .60m. above the chapel floor, the width is 2.30m. (central recess 1.30m.), and the depth is .65m.

Much of the east wall is also quarried away, but two small fragments of painted scenes in the top register remain below the ceiling. The southern half includes a statue niche for a single figure. It measures 1.00m. wide x .45m. deep x 1.80m. high, with a sill height of .65m. It has no jambs but, like the larger niche in the north wall, shows signs of being plastered and painted in a creamy colour with scattered red spots. Still clearly visible in the niche, although much damaged, is a life-size male figure, presumably the tomb owner.

The Shrine

The eastern side of the north wall of the chapel opens into the long shrine area which measures 13.20m. N-S x 2.80m. E-W and has the same ceiling and floor levels as the chapel. The entrance to the shrine is defined on either side by two engaged pillars, measuring .55m. N-S x .15m. E-W, which were originally connected at the top by a lintel that is now completely broken. 1.20m. north of the entrance on the west wall the outline of another engaged pillar, .50m. N-S x .10m. E-W, is visible at the floor level.

As in the chapel, the shrine is cleanly cut in good rock requiring little plaster to give a smooth, flat surface for decoration. Here, also, all walls were painted and the scenes are clearly discernible on the portions of walls which remain. As with other areas of this tomb, the walls have been deliberately cut to obtain good quality stone blocks, but floor and ceiling outlines are still distinct, providing accurate measurements. The west wall, from the entrance to the smaller false door at the northern end of the shrine, is now almost completely gone. The east wall has also been quarried into, particularly at the northern end and in the central part where this activity broke through into the shrine of the adjacent tomb M21.

In the west wall are two false doors cut in the mother rock. The southern and larger one is almost completely broken except for the lintel and fragmentary parts at floor level of the jambs, the platforms and the central recess. It measures 3.30m. wide x 3.40m. high. The lintel, projecting from the wall just below the ceiling, has exactly the same line as the outer jambs at the floor level. A platform 1.30m. wide x .20m. high is cut in front of each jamb on either side of the central recess. The central recess forms a niche .60m. square which, like the platforms, has a height of .20m. above floor level. It is large enough to have contained a life-size statue. Traces of plaster remain on the underside of the lintel, and fragments on the jambs and central recess indicate that they were painted in red and black, perhaps to simulate red granite. This false door may be presumed to have belonged to the tomb owner himself, both by virtue of its size and because the main burial chamber belonging to Sloping Passage II, lies directly beneath it.

The smaller false door at the extreme northern end of the west wall has completely disappeared below the drum, which shows signs of having been painted in red and black. The upper part is well preserved and retains most of the scenes and inscriptions on its plastered and painted surface, except on the right outer jamb where only sparse traces of colour are visible. This false door measures 2.50m. wide x 3.00m. high and has a platform 2.75m. wide x .20m. high directly in front of it. Exactly at the SE corner of this platform is cut Shaft IV, probably belonging to the wife of the tomb owner.

In the NE corner of the shrine there are indications of the beginning of another shaft, where an area 1.00m. square has been excavated to a depth of .35m. Only the upper half of the north wall still retains its painted surface. On the east wall one small section at the southern end was not cut away, and this still has scenes and inscriptions which cover the full height of the wall. To the north of this, below the ceiling and above the quarried parts, a long strip, forming the top register of the scenes, has partially survived.

IV BURIAL APARTMENTS

Figs. 1 – 5.

Inside the Chapel

Three vertical shafts and one sloping passage are cut into the floor of the tomb. All of the burial chambers are oriented N-S, and all were found plundered.

I In the SW corner of the chapel is cut a vertical shaft with a mouth 1.10m. square and a depth of 3.55m. The entrance to the burial chamber opens in the north wall at the floor of the shaft and measures 1.10m. wide x 1.10m. high. A rectangular burial chamber is 2.30m. N-S x 1.50m. E-W x 1.10m. high. Both it and the shaft are well cut.

II A sloping passage, cut with great precision, lies approximately in the centre of the chapel in front of and slightly to the west of the entrance. This passage is unusual in that while it terminates in an antechamber leading to a burial chamber with a burial pit, all complete and well cut, in the NW corner of the antechamber is found a vertical shaft leading to a second complete and well executed burial chamber and burial pit. It may be that the sloping passage was used as a device to extend northward in order to locate the burial chamber of the tomb owner beneath his large false door in the west wall of the shrine, concluding in a vertical shaft which is more typical in this cemetery during Dynasty V. It could also be that a second shaft, concealed within the first one, was intended to provide a more secure burial. The adjacent tomb,

M23, also of the late Fifth Dynasty, has an almost identical arrangement in its main burial apartment.

A vertical drop of .20m. leads to a large horizontal step 1.60m. long x 1.00m. wide. At the northern edge of this step is cut the mouth of the passage which measures 1.60m. E-W x 1.50m. N-S. A vertical drop of .95m. ends at a floor with a downward slope of 5°. In the north wall, the entrance to the sloping passage is defined by two jambs, .20m. wide x 1.10m. high. The passage itself has a width of .95m., a height of 1.10m., and descends in one slope at a 30° angle for 5.55m. In the centre of the floor and running the entire length of the passage is a square-cut channel, .30m. wide x .15m. deep. The entire passage is extremely well cut, all surfaces being smooth and flat.

At the bottom of this passage is an almost rectangular antechamber 3.90m. N-S x 2.25m. E-W at the north wall x 1.50m. high. In the floor of the antechamber is cut a broad and irregularly-shaped step, .55m. high, which leads down to the burial chamber cut in the west wall. This large burial chamber has an irregular shape, measuring 4.10m. N-S (maximum) x 3.25m. E-W at the south wall, and having a convexly curved ceiling with a central height of 1.60m. Although obviously unfinished in parts, it contains a meticulously cut and smoothly finished burial pit. This is defined by a perimeter upstand .15m. thick and measures 2.25m. x .75m. x .85m. total depth, the bottom being .40m. below the floor level. The interior shows signs of having been plastered.

In the NE corner of the antechamber is found a vertical shaft measuring 1.15m. N-S x 1.25m. E-W x 7.10m. deep. Behind its mouth in the east wall a recess 1.15m. wide x .30m. deep is cut the full height of the chamber. At the floor of the shaft the entrance to a second burial chamber is cut in the south wall. It measures 1.20m. wide x 1.50m. high. The burial chamber is very well cut and measures 4.30m. N-S x 1.40m. E-W x 1.55m. high, the ceiling being curved at the south end. Into the west wall is cut a very large recess having the same ceiling height as the burial chamber, but a higher floor level. It measures 3.30m. N-S x 2.10m. E-W x 1.35m. high. Into the floor of the recess is cut a well preserved burial pit 2.10m. x .80m. x 1.00m. deep which is defined by a perimeter upstand .20m. thick, the bottom of the pit being .80m. below the floor level of the recess. Three large pieces of dressed stone, all having the same thickness of .20m., were found in the chamber; probably they are parts of the lid belonging to this burial pit. Although plundered, pieces of the mummy and mummy wrappings were scattered in the chamber, including an almost perfectly preserved leg and a cartonnage hand-cover, as well as rope and a small fragment of a basket.

III In the NE corner of the chapel is cut a vertical shaft with a mouth 1.10m. square and a depth of 4.00m., although the floor is sloping and very incomplete, with uncut rock left in the eastern half. The entry to the burial chamber is cut in the west wall and measures 1.05m. wide x 1.00m. high. The rectangular-shaped burial chamber is oriented N-S and measures 1.35m. on the south wall, 1.10m. on the north wall, 2.40m. N-S, and 1.00m. high. A burial pit contiguous to the north and west walls measures 2.00m. x .90m. x .30m. deep. The chamber is well cut and in good condition.

IV This especially well cut vertical shaft is situated at the SE corner of the platform lying in front of the false door at the northern end of the shrine. Presumably it belongs to the wife of the tomb owner. It has a mouth measuring

1.15m. square and is 4.90m. deep. An entrance cut in the north wall at the floor of the shaft is .90m. wide x 1.30m. high. One step, .15m. high, leads down to an almost rectangular burial chamber which is 3.00m. N-S x 1.45m. along the south wall and 1.60m. along the north wall. Contiguous with the west wall is a burial pit cut into the floor which measures 1.80m. x .80m. It has a sloping floor with an average depth of .50m., and is defined by a perimeter upstand which is .10m. thick along the west side and .20m. thick on the other three sides.

Outside the Chapel

Nine burial pits were excavated in the floor of the forecourt area, all of which were found plundered.

(a) This small and incomplete pit is adjacent to the low fence in the western part of the forecourt. It has a rectangular mouth 1.00m. N-S x .85m. E-W. Work was abandoned at a shallow depth upon running into tomb M25, which is cut in the east wall of the forecourt of neighbouring tomb M23. (No section plans are given for Pit a.)

(b) In the western side of the forecourt, opposite the entrance to tomb M27, a small vertical pit has a step along the length of its eastern side, which is 1.00m. x .15m. x .35m. high. Its mouth measures 1.00m. N-S x .85m. E-W and it is 1.55m. deep. There is no burial chamber as such, but in the east wall is cut a recess at the level of the shaft floor. This recess is .80m. long x .90m. wide and has a curved roof measuring .65m. high at the entry.

(c) In front of the western side of the façade, a section of the low fence was cut away in order to excavate a small vertical pit with a mouth .80m. square and a depth of 1.75m. In the north wall an opening .60m. wide x .70m. high leads to a small shapeless chamber. It measures 1.10m. E-W x .55m. N-S with a ceiling sloping from .70m. at the entrance to .50m. at the north wall.

(d) West of the doorway and contiguous with the façade is a vertical pit .80m. square and 2.10m. deep. An entry, .50m. wide x .90m. high, cut in the north wall opens into a long narrow chamber 1.85m. N-S x .70m. E-W at the north wall x .90m. high. A niche, .30m. wide x .20m. deep x .65m. high with a sloping roof, is cut into the north wall at a height of .10m. above floor level.

(e) In the corner between the entrances of M22 and M27 is a vertical pit .95m. square x 2.10m. deep. Into the north wall is cut a rectangular burial chamber 1.45m. N-S x 1.20m. E-W x .65m. high. Although cleanly cut with sharp angles, the walls, floor and ceiling are uneven, and perhaps unfinished. Above this shaft in the east wall, which also forms the façade of tomb M27, is a small sculpted but uninscribed false door. It measures .60m. wide x .80m. high.

(f) Against the east wall between the doorways of tombs M27 and M28 is a vertical pit with a mouth .90m. square and a depth of 1.90m. The floor of the shaft is uneven and rough. A burial chamber cut into the south wall at a SE angle is curved and completely shapeless. At its widest point it measures .80m., with a length of 1.30m. and a height of .90m. This pit is roughly finished and a false door above it was left in painted outline in a shallow recess which measures .50m. wide x 1.60m. high.

(g) In front of the wall between the doorways of tombs M28 and M29 is a vertical pit with a mouth .90m. square and a depth of 2.45m. A small area of rock in the SE corner of the shaft floor has been left uncut. There is no burial chamber, but in the west wall is a recess with two roof levels of .60m. and .35m. high, a width of .65m. and a total length of .35m.

(h) Immediately to the south of the entry to tomb M29 is a vertical pit 1.10m. N-S x 1.00m. E-W x 2.55m. deep. Along the north side of the mouth and partly intruding on the entrance to M29, is cut a large and deep step, .90m. x .70m. x .80m. high. Just .10m. below the bottom level of this step, at a depth of .90m. a shallow ledge or niche is cut the full width of the east wall of the shaft, measuring 1.10m. x .20m. x .65m. high. At the floor of the shaft in the west wall, a doorway .80m. wide and .85m. high is defined by two narrow jambs .10m. thick. This gives entry to a burial chamber 2.10m. N-S x 1.20m. E-W x .85m. high.

(i) At the southern end of the east wall is a shallow vertical pit whose mouth measures 1.10m. N-S x 1.00m. E-W. The shaft reaches a total depth of 2.10m., but the cutting in the lower half is rough and incomplete, as is the sloping floor. Into the west wall a burial chamber is cut at a SW angle. It is rectangular in shape with a level floor and ceiling, and measures 2.10m. long x .90m. wide x .70m. high.

V SCENES, STATUES AND INSCRIPTIONS

In spite of the fact that M22 was cut in an area with considerably better rock formation than other areas on the mountain, the quality of rock is not consistent throughout the tomb. While it was possible to obtain smooth surfaces for relief on the thicknesses of the entrance, and to cut statues in the mother rock inside the chapel, the rest of the walls had to be covered with a thin and very smooth layer of gypsum plaster and to be decorated in painting.

The Entrance

Pl. 5; Figs. 6, 7.

Nothing is now visible on the façade which is much eroded and has partly collapsed. However, both thicknesses of the doorway still retain part of their decoration which is executed in sunk relief.

THE RIGHT DOOR THICKNESS

The tomb owner stands facing right, i.e., towards the outside of the tomb. Most of his figure has disappeared, but enough remains to show that he wears a short, pointed skirt, and holds the staff with his left hand and the sekhem sceptre in his right. The legend that was probably written above his head is now completely missing. Standing close behind him is his wife, with her left hand presumably resting on his left shoulder. She wears a long, tight dress and anklets. The inscriptions above her read: *ḥmt [.f] rḫ(t) nswt ḥm(t)-nṯr Ḥwt-ḥr [Ḥknw]-Mwt* 'his wife, the acquaintance of the king, the priestess of Hathor, Hekenu-Mut' (compare with the opposite thickness).

THE LEFT DOOR THICKNESS

This probably contained a representation identical to that on the opposite thickness. But while the woman's figure is better preserved on this side of the doorway, only the heel of the husband's figure and the back of the sekhem sceptre are now visible. The woman wears a long wig with a tress falling over the front of the collar, a long, tight dress with two shoulder straps, and anklets. The inscriptions above her are badly damaged, but may be restored as follows: . . . *ḥm(t)-[nṯr Ḥwt-ḥr] Ḥknw-[Mwt]* '. . . the priestess of Hathor, Hekenu-Mut' (compare with the opposite thickness).

The Chapel

The south wall to the east of the entrance

has collapsed to a height of less than 1.25m. from the ground, thus leaving no information on the decoration of this section, unless of course some of the fragmentary scenes found in the debris and published here originally belonged to it.

SOUTH WALL – WEST OF THE ENTRANCE

Pls. 1, 3 a – c; Figs. 8 – 11.

The upper half of the wall is occupied by a scene of Hesi-Min and his wife receiving offerings. The couple sit facing left on a chair with bulls' legs and low, cushioned back. Underneath it stands their hound. The man wears a shoulder-length (?) wig, a collar and a short, pointed skirt. His left hand rests opened, palm downward, on his lap, while his right reaches forward towards an offering table before him, loaded with twelve loaves of bread. Close beside him sits his wife with her right hand resting on his right shoulder and her left on her lap. She has a broad collar, anklets and a bracelet on her left wrist, and wears a long, tight dress with two shoulder straps which is decorated with an elaborate bead-net pattern. Above them the partly preserved inscription reads: *rḫ nswt mrr nb.f . . . Ḥzjj-Mnw ḥmt.f . . .* 'the acquaintance of the king, the beloved of his lord . . . Hesi-Min. His wife . . .'. Above the offering table is written: *ḫ3 šs*[55]*ḫ3 t(?) ḫ3 ḥnqt ḫ3 k3(?) ḫ3 3pd* 'a thousand of linen, a thousand of bread (?), a thousand of beer, a thousand of oxen (?) and a thousand of fowl'; and the text continues under the table: *ḫ3 mnḫt* 'a thousand of clothes'.

The rest of the wall in front of the couple and the offering table is divided into four registers of equal height, with the two uppermost divided in their right part into two subsidiary registers each. The scenes here are crowded and full of internal details, all executed with great finesse. The rest of the wall below the seated figures of Hesi-Min and his wife is divided into two further registers (i.e., nos. 5 and 6), which probably extended across the entire width of this section of the wall.

Register I. The area to the right is divided into two subsidiary registers where food and drinks are depicted. Various sorts of fruits and vegetables (not always easily identifiable), plucked geese, and pieces of meat are placed on and under small tables (or perhaps trays on stands), or in bowls and baskets, with or without covers. Included also are jars of drinks of different shapes, mostly with lids and some with spouts. The food and drinks are arranged in alternating groups, beginning with food in the top subsidiary register and with drinks in the lower one.

The left section of the register is occupied by a row of offering bearers bringing more items to Hesi-Min and his wife. All the men wear the short, tight skirt knotted at the waist. The first two carry between them a small table laden with food. The third man holds some lotus flowers and buds in his left hand while supporting a basket on his shoulder with his right. The fourth man leads a small animal (probably a calf) on a rope. The fifth bearer carries a tray on his left shoulder.

Register II. As is the case with Register I, the right section of the two subsidiary registers is also occupied by alternating groups of food and drinks. But the first object near the hands of the tomb owner and his wife is a stand supporting a spouted jar and two ewers in basins, both facing towards the seated figures, probably one being for each individual.[56] The offering bearers in the left part of the register are also dressed in short, tight skirts. The first carries lotus flowers and buds in his left hand and supports with the other hand a tray of food on his right shoulder. The second man carries a container of food (?) in each hand, while the third lifts a large bowl with both hands. Only the head and right shoulder are now visible of the fourth bearer, who turns his face backwards.

Register III. The inscriptions to the right of the register explain the action of the represented men: *sḫp stpt n k3 hrw [nb]*[57] 'bringing the choice of food for the ka every day'. All the offering bearers face right and are dressed in the same style as the ones depicted in the upper registers. The first man holds a goose in his right hand while wringing its neck with his left. The second man carries two birds in each hand, and the third bearer lifts two birds in his left hand while holding a lotus bouquet in his right. Of the fourth man only the hands remain, and he apparently carries the foreleg of an ox.

Register IV. Immediately in front of Hesi-Min and his wife is a male figure presenting them with lotus flowers. This theme appears in a number of tomb scenes, yet they differ in many respects from our example. Whether the tomb owner sits alone,(58) or with his wife,(59) he is usually presented with one lotus flower. In our case the couple are offered at least three, possibly four flowers, judging by the number of stems.(60) The elements of composition here agree with other similar scenes: the upper area is occupied by stacks of food and the lower one by music and dancing.(61) However, our scene is to be differentiated from the others by the presence of an offering table before the seated figures. This, in turn, may account for another clear difference. While the tomb owners are usually shown already receiving the lotus flowers, Hesi-Min is not, possibly because his hand is extended towards the offering table.(62) It may be reasonable to think that the presentation of the lotus was a later addition, not planned in the original layout of the scene. No inscriptions accompany the small figure holding the lotus flowers, but by analogy with individuals shown in a similar attitude in other tombs, he may have been the tomb owner's son.(63)

To the left of the offering table is a female harpist, who perhaps headed a team of musicians and dancers.(64) She holds the neck of the instrument against her shoulder, with the soundbox, which is decorated with the *wḏ3t* – eye,(65) placed on the ground. All the details showing the attachment of the strings to the neck, and the use of the wooden pegs are well drawn.(66) Behind the harpist is written *sqr* 'striking' or 'playing'. As the wall below and to the left of this word is damaged, the caption may have originally been *sqr (m) bnt* 'playing (on) the harp.'(67) The rest of the register is now missing.

Register V. The register begins with the figure of a herdsman wearing a loin-cloth and leading a hornless ox on a rope, while touching its forehead with his right hand. The ox is captioned *rn ng3w* 'young ox'(68) and is adorned with an elaborate collar, identical with those shown in the mastabas of Ptah-hetep and Mereru-ka.(69) A second attendant places his left hand on this animal's rump, and holds with his right a rope attached to a long-horned ox which is labelled as *nr* (for *rn*)(70) *jw3* 'young ox'. The third man in the register is only partly preserved, yet seems particularly interesting. Although his feet, like those of other individuals represented on this wall (with the exception of Hesi-Min and his wife), face right, this herdsman made a complete turn of his body so that he faces left. He apparently received a head-butt from the ox behind him, of which only the horn is now visible. The man, whose hair is unusually depicted as standing on end (perhaps as a result of the accident or the fright (?)), is trying to push back the animal with his left hand.

Register VI. The lower part of this wall, as that of the neighbouring one, is in a bad state of preservation, but enough remains of the paintings to reconstruct the subject matter. The right section is occupied by a bullfighting scene, where one bull has tossed his opponent. The herdsman, described as *jmj-r ṯzt Q3j-Mnw* 'the master drover, Kai-Min', lifts his hand high holding a long stick. He is presumably the same as *Q3j-Mnw* depicted on the adjacent west wall.

As bullfighting is never depicted in the wall decoration of the Memphite cemeteries,(71) this would be the earliest example so far attested, according to our dating of the tomb. It is regrettable that the caption above the animals has suffered some damage, which renders its reading uncertain. Yet the importance of this theme in the wall decoration at El-Hawawish may be gauged from its representation in tombs H24 and H26, where the tomb owners are said to be *m33* 'watching' the fight.[72] The following is simply an attempt at translating the partly preserved text in M22, which forms four horizontal lines:[73] (1) *mj jnjj.ṯn jr(.j) njwtjw jw m33.ṯn (2) sm3.n.f sw [wḥʿ ?] .n(.j) ḥr.f . . . sp.n(.j) jm.f (3) wḥm [šzp ?] .f ḥn.ṯn (4) m ʿnḫ* '(1) Come and bring the townsmen to (me). You (will) see (2) that he (can) kill him, whom (I) [released ?] at him, and I . . . on him. (3) He (will) receive (assails) again, on your (4) life.'

COMMENTS

(a) The first sign to the right is certainly *m*, probably for *mj*  'come'.

(b) *jr(.j)* is likely to be a dative 'to me', i.e. 'to where I am'. The suffix *.j* appears to be regularly omitted in the text.

(c) I take *sm3.n.f* at the beginning of line 2 to express an action simultaneously spoken of and performed (Gardiner, *Grammar*, § 414:5).

(d) The first incomplete sign after the long lacuna in line 2 might possibly be , without the oar, as is usual in the Old Kingdom (Fischer, *Calligraphy*, 37). This might be the determinative for *wḥʿ* 'release' (see, e.g., Petrie, *Athribis*, pl. 7).

(e) In line 2 the letter *n*, after both *wḥʿ* (?) and . . . *sp* may suggest two *sḏm.n.f* forms (or relative forms), with the suffix *.j* omitted. In either case the form is followed by a preposition + suffix.

(f) The first lacuna in line 3 may be filled with *m*, of *wḥm*.

(g) The sign after *wḥm* seems to be  *šzp*.

(h) The last words in line 3 and that of line 4 seem to be the formula 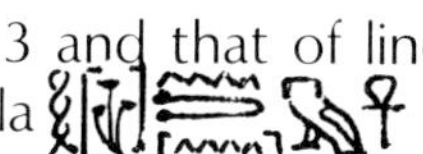. It is likely that the suffix *.ṯn* in the formula refers to the townsmen. In this case, the meaning would appear to be closer to Montet's rendering 'on your life', probably in the sense of a pledge rather than an adjuration (Montet, *Vie privée*, 171-72), than to Erman's translation 'as hard as you can' (Erman, *Reden*, 8).

Immediately to the left is the beginning of what was most probably the scene of a desert hunt. We can only see a hound attacking an animal (?) in an environment represented by a wavy line and small shrubs, indicating the nature of the desert. As this wavy line seems exactly in the centre of the register, it is reasonable to think that the lower half of the register was occupied by a second and similar line, as is the case in the mastabas of Ptah-hetep and Seshem-nefer.[74]

WEST WALL

Pls. 2, 3d; Figs. 12, 13.

The scenes on this wall can be divided into three subjects. From top: (A) spear fishing; (B) bringing the master drovers for the count; (C) herding animals.

(A) Spear fishing. This scene occupies most of the height of the wall, leaving only a narrow wall space for both (B) and (C). The tomb owner, facing right, is shown in a papyrus boat, wearing a collar and a sporting tunic fastened at the waist with a belt. The posture of his raised right arm and lowered left allows the spear to point downwards at an angle of 22°, and creates a better movement than the traditional one of the Old Kindgom where the spear is held almost horizontally.[75] One wonders whether the painted details on the spear represent imitation of reed jointing,[76] or whether the spear was actually made of this plant which was no doubt abundant in the marshland. Nothing can now be seen of the speared fish and, judging by the space available, it is possible that no papyrus thicket was originally painted.[77]

In front of Hesi-Min is a male figure designated as *z3.f smsw ḥm-nṯr Mnw Nj-ʿnḫ-Mnw* 'his eldest son, the priest of Min, Ni-ankh-Min'. This son is shown in the same attitude as that of his father, but his spear points at a steeper angle towards the river.(78) The artist probably had more freedom in showing the son's efforts than his father's, hence the traditional fish in the column of water before the tomb owner(79) (now missing in our scene). Beside Hesi-Min stands a woman, most probably his wife, with fragmentary inscription above her which may read: *[ḥmt] .f . . . [Špsjt]-k3w*(80) 'his [wife] . . . [Shepsit]-kau'. She wears a collar, a long, tight dress with two shoulder straps and anklets and, as expected, she is depicted to the left of Hesi-Min, so that her figure does not hide any part of his. The three occupants of the boat stand on a broad wooden board, which would give them better footing than the softer papyrus, and at the same time help distribute the weight more evenly on the vessel. Such a board is regularly represented in fishing and fowling scenes where the tomb owner had to be standing,(81) but wood grain of the board is rarely shown,(82) or at least it is not reproduced in excavation reports of painted tombs. Below the stern of the boat, water weeds, *potamogeton lucens*, are floating, and on them sit a frog and a grasshopper. While the former is usually depicted among the weeds,(83) the latter is less frequently shown.(84) Behind the main boat and partly beneath its stern is a small papyrus boat of the type used by fishermen, with its stern higher than the prow.(85) One fisherman is aboard, sitting on a reed seat with his equipment placed behind him. In his left hand he holds a line with multiple hooks which have already caught a fish, probably a *clarias anguillaris*.(86) The raised right hand of the fisherman probably grasps a club (now almost totally damaged) with which he is about to strike the fish as it rises out of the water. According to Vandier the technique of using this club in fishing was restricted to the Memphite region, but never attested in Upper Egypt.(87) This association with the Memphite art is of some interest.(88)

The water beneath the papyrus boats is painted in blue without the conventional wavy lines.(89) In addition to the above-mentioned hooked fish, two others are swimming: a *mugil* to the right and a *mormyrus niloticus* at the centre.(90) The fish, although partly damaged, are very well rendered and shaded coloration of them appears to have been attempted, using different degrees of red/orange to yellow colour. Present also are a hippopotamus and a crocodile. But instead of attacking each other,(91) the former is occupied with the boat above it,(92) while the latter has just caught a fish.(93) The details of the crocodile's skin are excellently rendered in yellow with brown lines.

The spaces in front of and behind the tomb owner are occupied by male figures who probably accompanied him on his fishing trip. They wear short wigs and, wherever it is possible to verify, short, tight skirts. The three men before Hesi-Min face left towards him. The first of them probably carries lotus flowers in his right hand (only the stems are now visible), the second a tray or basket of food, but what the third is carrying is unclear.

Four lines of hieroglyphs labelling the scene are also inscribed in this area: (1) *stjt mḥt ᶜ3 wrt n . . . (2) stjt mḥt . . . (3) š3w . . . (4) m pḥww* '(1) spearing a very great catch of fish for . . . (2) spearing a catch of fish [in?] . . . (3) the marshlands . . . (4) in the far north.' Above the spear are the signs: . . . *k3 hrw nb*, which by analogy with a similar inscription on the south wall of the chapel and the north wall of the shrine may be completed as *[sḫp stpt n] k3 hrw nb* 'bringing the choice of food for the ka every day.' Although the scene here portrays fishing, such an inscription is still likely since the men immediately above it carry food other than fish.

Behind Hesi-Min are five men in two registers, all facing right. The two in the top register each hold a two-pronged spear in the left hand and a fish in the right. The first fish, which is better preserved, may be a *clarias* of some sort. Before the man in the front is written: *z3.f Nṯrj-rn-Mnw* 'his son, Netjeri-ren-Min', but only the sign *f* remains from the label for the man at the rear. This may be the suffix *.f* in *z3.f* 'his son'. Can this man be *Nb-ʿnḫ-Mnw* who appears opposite his brother *Nṯrj-rn-Mnw* on their mother's false door?

Three men are depicted in the lower register (notice that no base line is drawn here), each holding a lotus flower and bud in his left hand and a fish in his right. The fish may tentatively be identified as *lates niloticus* and two *clarias anguillaris*.(94) The first man is described as *z3.f Nfr-s[. . .]-Mnw* 'his son, Nefer-s[. . .]-Min', but no names are given for the second and third men. Instead, a legend is written above them which continues behind the third man: *jnt n mḥt jn ḥmw-k3* 'bringing the catch of fish by the ka-servants'.

(B) Bringing the master drovers for the count. This register is badly damaged, but enough remains to give the general picture. From right: Two scribes are squatting, facing right as do all the other figures. Each has the word *zš* 'scribe' written above his head. Immediately to the right is the title *jmj-r pr* 'steward', referring to a man whose figure has survived only in small fragments of colour (not in our drawing). Holders of this title are frequently shown presenting the counts to the tomb owners.(95) Behind the scribes is the *jmj-r ṯzt Q3j-Mnw* 'master drover, Kai-Min' who may well be the same individual represented in the bottom register on the south wall. Wearing a short, pointed skirt, he steps forward and raises both hands holding a stick. Following him is a second supervisor, bowing slightly, who holds a stick in his left hand, while his right is probably placed on the head of the man behind him; the latter bends forward much further and has his hands by his sides.(96) Four herdsmen are then shown squatting and bending forward slightly. The first three have their left hands placed on their laps, while that of the fourth is on his chest. At the left side of the register is a herdsman holding an ox on a rope, which is followed by a second herdsman wearing a short, tight skirt, who places his left hand on the animal's back while touching its tail with his right.(97)

The whole scene is labelled: *jnt jmjw-r ṯzwt r ḥs[b] nw [pr]-ḏt*(98) 'bringing the master drovers of the estate to the count.'(99)

(C) Herding animals. This register has suffered the most. It shows live stock, probably goats, in the front, oxen at the rear, shrubs of different sizes growing from the ground, and herdsmen. The man to the right has almost completely disappeared, the one in the middle places his left hand on the animal's rump and lifts his right which holds a stick. The third herdsman at the extreme left has a bag hanging from his stick which he carries over his shoulder.

Only the end of the text describing this scene has survived; its meaning is therefore uncertain: . . . *jnw nw pr-ḏ[t]* '. . .(the herdsmen? and?) the produce of the estate'.

NORTH WALL

Pl. 6a.

This wall has been quarried away from near the ceiling to a height of about 1m. from the ground. Any scenes and inscriptions which probably covered the wall have, therefore, completely disappeared. Only patches of colours from the upper frieze can now be seen on pieces of rock projecting down from the ceiling, being left unquarried.

Damaged portions of two life-size statues, cut in the mother rock, remain in a statue niche. Both survive only below the knees and represent a male and female, presumably the tomb owner and his wife. As only one leg of the male figure is attached to the rear wall of the niche, which is smooth and plastered in the place where the second leg should be, it may be assumed that the man had his left foot stepping forward. A small protrusion of rock, elevated above the plastered floor of the niche, may well have formed part of the left foot. To the right of the man stands a female figure, her two feet close together, wearing a long dress and most probably anklets, of which traces of colour are still visible. The niche itself was plastered and painted in a creamy colour with scattered large red spots.

EAST WALL

Pl. 6b; Fig. 14.

The right section of the wall is occupied by a single life-size statue of the tomb owner (?), in a statue niche, entirely cut in the mother rock. The niche is plastered and painted in a creamy colour with red spots. Although the general posture of the statue is clear, with its hands by the side and the legs close together, all the details of the body and face have completely disappeared. It is possible that these were not originally cut in the rock, but were added in thick plaster, which has since fallen away.

The left section of the wall has mostly been quarried away, with only a portion of the upper part of the wall still in place. Two fragments of scenes here and the remains of text: . . . *k3t jn* . . .'. . .work by. . .', indicate that the subject of decoration was the workshop. The left fragment shows a man raising his hand with a hammer (?). Judging by the position of his hand, he was probably facing right, and perhaps engaged in chiselling a statue.(100) Next to him are two men facing left and wearing short wigs. They apparently blow air into a furnace using long pipes, one of which is still visible. In such scenes one expects to find another pair of men in a similar position facing this one.(101)

In the centre of the wall are the remains of two pairs of men facing each other. Each man has an upraised arm, possibly beating metal to shape vessels, one of which is shown above them. It may be observed that the men do not hold in their hands the round stones usually used as hammers.(102) Above the men the remains of the word *sqr* 'beating'(103) is visible.

The Shrine

THE WEST WALL

Pl. 4; Fig. 15.

This wall, except at its northern end, has been quarried away from above the floor level to just a few centimetres below the roof. Therefore, while the architectural plan and section of this part of the tomb are easily perceived, all scenes and inscriptions, apart from those on the northern false door, have disappeared. It remains possible, however, that some of the loose fragments found in the debris originally belonged to this wall. Most of these fragments show parts of offerings and/or offering bearers, and these are sometimes represented on the west walls near the false doors.(104) The north wall of the shrine is another possible origin for these fragments, but not the east wall, judging by the surviving sections of the subjects depicted there.

The False Doors

Two false doors were cut in the west wall of the shrine. The southern one, which is of larger dimensions than the northern,(105) has, like other parts of the wall, been quarried away, except for its upper lintel and the lower section of the door. This includes two offering platforms left in the mother rock in front of the right and left jambs.(106) In other cases where two false doors decorate the west wall, it is usual for the southern one to belong to the tomb owner and the northern to his wife.(107) This seems almost certain in our case, for not only is the southern false door the larger of the two, but also it is positioned above the burial chamber of Sloping Passage II which is most probably the main burial apartment in this tomb. The northern false door lies above the burial chamber of Shaft IV, the second in size in the tomb.

THE NORTHERN FALSE DOOR

The upper lintel (A) with the outer jambs (B, C) form a continuous frame for the false door, separating it from the scenes which once existed on the neighbouring walls.[108] Both the upper (A) and lower (G) lintels are each occupied by one line of large hieroglyphs,[109] while the outer jambs, judging by the remaining part of the left one, were decorated with the figures of offering bearers.[110] The left and right margins (E, F) adjacent to the panel (D) portray relations of the tomb owner,[111] and the central niche (J) was left undecorated.[112] These features were employed predominantly in the Fifth Dynasty, although they started earlier and continued in the Sixth Dynasty.

Scenes and Inscriptions

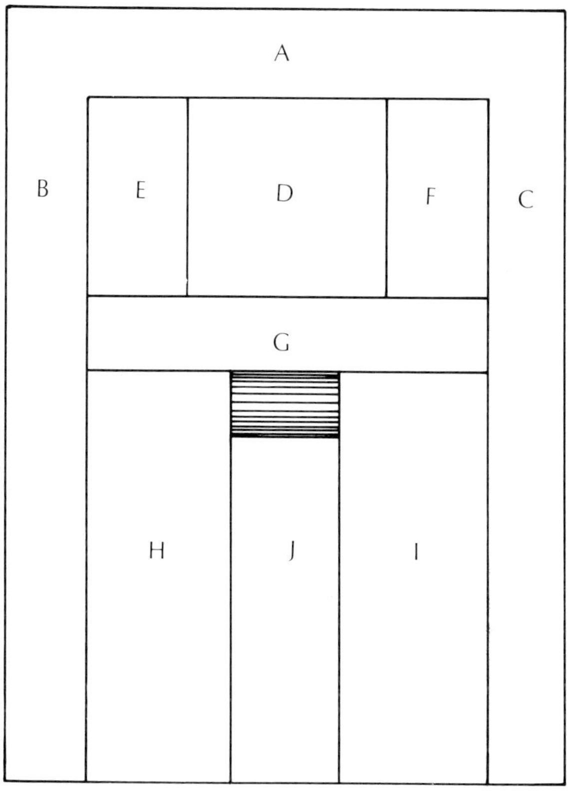

A: From left: *wr mḏ Šmʿ jmj-r k3t nt nswt jmj-r z3w Šmʿ* . . . 'the greatest of the ten of Upper Egypt, the overseer of the work of the king, the overseer of the phyles of Upper Egypt . . .'. The lacuna at the end of the line was most probably occupied by Hesi-Min's name.

B: A male offering bearer is represented facing right towards the centre of the false door. He wears a short, tight skirt and carries a jar (?) hanging from a rope in his right hand while supporting with his left a tray of food on his shoulder. Above him is written: *ḥm-k3* 'the ka-servant', and before him his name is given as *ʿnḫw* 'Ankhu'.[113] The lower part of this jamb as well as the whole of the opposite jamb (C) have disappeared.

D: The tomb owner, facing right, sits on a chair with bulls' legs. He wears a shoulder-length wig and a collar, but the rest of his body, except for the lower part of the legs which are clearly separated, is completely missing. Facing him is the small figure of his wife wearing a long wig, a choker, a broad collar and a long, tight dress with shoulder straps. Her feet are only partly visible, the rest being hidden behind her husband's so that nothing may obscure his figure. She holds lotus flowers in her left hand, while her right is extended forward, perhaps touching her husband's knee, or presenting him with lotus flowers or with some kind of offering. Above her is written: *rḫ(t) nswt Špsjt-k3w* 'the acquaintance of the king, Shepsit-kau'. The inscriptions in front of the man read: *rḫ nswt Ḥz[jj]-Mnw* 'the acquaintance of the king, Hesi-Min', and those behind him: *jm3ḫw ḫr nṯr ʿ3* 'the honoured one before the great god'.

There does not seem to be any space left on the panel for the offering table usually depicted in this place. It is interesting to compare this scene with that on the northern false door in the tomb of *Sšm-nfr III*, where, despite the fact that the wife is not represented, no offering table is shown.[114]

E: A male figure facing right and wearing a short, tight skirt holds a goose in his right hand while wringing its neck with his left. He is labelled as *z3.f Nb-ʿnḫ-Mnw* 'his son, Neb-ankh-Min'.

F: A male figure facing left apparently burns

incense. He is designated as *z3.f Nṯrj-rn-Mnw* 'his son, Netjeri-ren-Min'.

G: From right: *wr [mḏ Šmʿ] jmj-[r k3]t [nt nswt] rḫ nswt ḥm-nṯr Mnw Ḥzj[j]-Mnw* 'the greatest of the ten of Upper Egypt, the overseer of the work of the king, the acquaintance of the king, the priest of Min, Hesi-Min'.

H: A standing figure of the tomb owner is facing right, holding a long staff, but only a section of the upper part of the body is now visible. He wears a collar and a bracelet on his left arm. Two horizontal lines of hieroglyphs give his titles and name: (1) *wr mḏ Šmʿ s[. . .] nswt (2) Ḥs[jj-Mnw]* '(1) the greatest of the ten of Upper Egypt, the . . . of the king, (2) Hesi-Min'.

I: A fragment of the figure of the tomb owner's wife faces left. She wears a collar and a bracelet on her right arm and holds a lotus flower close to her nostrils. One horizontal line (1) and another vertical line (2) give her titles and name: (1) *ḥm(t)-nṯr Ḥwt-ḥr nb(t) nht Špsjt-[k3w] (2) ḥm(t) nṯr Nt*[115] '(1) the priestess of Hathor lady of the sycamore, Shepsit-kau, (2) the priestess of Neith'.

NORTH WALL

Pl. 7a; Fig. 16.

The lower section of this wall has been quarried away, and the upper section has suffered a great deal from the effect of the salt. The remaining scenes are in a very bad state of preservation.

Hesi-Min in heroic dimensions stands facing left, and wearing a broad collar, bracelets, and the panther's skin. He holds the long staff at an angle with his right hand, while his left hangs by his side. As the rock below this is missing, it is impossible to determine whether he also held the sekhem sceptre. The fragmentary signs above his head probably listed his titles, of which one can now read only: *jmj-r k3[t nt nswt?]* 'the overseer of the works [of the king]'. Only one hieroglyphic sign remains in front of his face, which could be the last of his name, *Ḥzjj-Mnw.*[116] Behind him are some signs which must have formed a vertical column of hieroglyphs. This now reads: *rḫ [nswt wr] mḏ Šmʿ* 'the acquaintance of the king, the greatest of the ten of Upper Egypt'.

The upper two registers of the wall scenes opposite the tomb owner's figure have survived, but are in a very bad state of preservation.

Register I. The top section was occupied by food offerings, of which the head of a hornless ox and a small food tray on a low stand are still recognisable. In the lower section three offering bearers face right towards the main figure. The last two of them wear short, tight skirts.

Register II. Between the standing figure of Hesi-Min and his staff we read: *z3.f smsw*[117] *[Nj-ʿnḫ]-Mnw* 'his eldest son, [Ni-ankh]-Min'. One would expect the small figure of the son to be depicted beneath this inscription, and judging by the direction of the hieroglyphic signs, he should be facing left, as does his father.

A small figure, labelled as *ḥm-k3* 'ka-servant', faces the tomb owner and presents him with a lotus flower. Following are two butchers at work, the one to the right pulls back the animal's foreleg with both hands, while his companion holds the same foreleg with his left hand and makes an incision (?) with a knife held in his right. Above them we read: *stpt n k3 hrw nb* 'the choice of food for the ka every day'.[118]

EAST WALL

Pls. 7b, 8; Figs. 17, 18.

This was certainly a most interesting wall, depicting many activities from daily life. It is unfortunate that with the exception of a relatively narrow section towards the southern end of the wall, near the entrance to the shrine, the rock has been quarried away, leaving only the upper part of the scenes, approximately 40cm. below the frieze. As a result we now have three registers of scenes in the southern part, but only one in the northern.

Register I. The scenes here represent a mixture of activities performed in marshland and agricultural land. They may be divided into various subjects: (A) cutting papyrus and building boats, (B) harvesting flax, (C) cattle herding, (D) cattle crossing the water, and (E) procession of animals (?).

(A) From right: A man bending forward carries a bundle of papyrus on his back. To the left of him are two men binding another bunch of the same plant by pulling a rope in opposite directions. Three men are then engaged in building a papyrus boat by tying the papyrus stems together with ropes. The effort they are putting into their work is obvious, and the first of them to the right is applying the weight of his body to the rope which passes under his foot.(119) Three rolls of rope appear above the men's heads. They seem to represent additional rolls to be used, rather than to form part of an inscription.(120) Further left are the heads of two men who must be working on the same boat, the man to the right being on the other side of the vessel. The inscription explaining the work is partly damaged, but may be restored to: *spt*(121) *m mḥt*(122) 'constructing (a boat) in the marshland'.(123)

(B) Two men facing each other bend over to harvest flax, while a third man carries a sheaf. Above them is written: *ḥwj mḥ*ᶜ 'pulling(124) the flax'. To the left of this group of men is another group of three, all facing right. Two of these are bending over to pull the plant, while the third holds an already cut bundle labelled: *ṯt* (for *ṯ3t*?)(125) *mḥ*ᶜ 'pulled flax'.(126) All the men wear the short, tight skirts, and are shown either with short hair, or even partly bald.

(C) Two cows are facing each other, with a suckling calf under the cow to the right and another calf between the two large animals. Above the cow to the left we read: *jdt* 'cow'. Behind her is a bull labelled as *k3* 'bull'. The cattle are probably in the marshes, judging by the small shrubs coming out of the ground; the same type of shrubs are depicted in the boat-building scene.

(D) Cattle are crossing the water, with herdsmen in papyrus boats preceding and following the herd. Three men are in the front boat, two engaged in moving the vessel using oars, while the third kneels in the stern, holding the foreleg of a young calf to assist him swimming and to entice the herd to follow. The movements of the men in the rear boat are less clear now, but we can distinguish a man standing in the stern, pushing the boat by using a long pole.

The caption above this scene has suffered a great deal of damage, but may be restored as follows:(127) *nrw pw w3ḥ [*ᶜ*.k ḥr mw w]r[t j]r šjj pw ntj ḥr mw jw[.f m] šp* 'O, this herdsman, may [your hand] endure upon the water,(128) [greatly], against that aquatic (creature) which is on the water (i.e. the crocodile). May [he] pass as if blind'.

(E) A herdsman, wearing a short, tight skirt places his hands on the rump and tail of an animal captioned: *m3* (or *m3-ḥḏ*?) 'oryx'. Although this may represent the rear of the procession of animals returning from the pasture,(129) the proximity of the scene to that of the cattle crossing the water, and the depiction of a shrub near the oryx's leg, may indicate that the herd is still near the grazing area.

Register II. Men are building a papyrus boat in the marshland. They are depicted in different postures, pulling the ropes to bind together the papyrus stems. The man on the right end of the boat is giving an order to his companions: *wn ṯn* 'hurry up'. The answer to this is badly erased.

Register III. This register is much higher than the other two on this wall. Only the representation of one large ship has survived the quarrying away of rock in the tomb. The ship is in full sail, the wind is sufficient, and accordingly the rowers are at rest. Standing in the cabin amidships is a large figure of a man holding a long staff; perhaps he is the tomb owner himself.[130] A man sits on the cabin roof with the sail ropes in hand. Immediately below him, and standing in the stern, are two steersmen, each holding a long pole to direct the boat.

VI FINDS

Human Remains

Pl. 9a, b.

A large amount of very disturbed and broken bones and linen bandages were scattered in the lower burial chamber of Sloping Passage II. Among these, however, a complete and wrapped leg was found. It is 1.01m. long, with the foot .26m. long. Although no resin had been used to mould the bandages of the leg into shape, this was certainly done for other parts of the body, as indicated by a large fragment of the wrappings of the left hand found amoung the mass of linen in the burial chamber. The bandages were modelled with care over the clenched hand, with all fingers defined, but not separated, except for the top of the thumb which is free. No plaster was used,[131] but a light brown paint was applied to the top of the hand and a red-brown to the nails (only that of the thumb remains).

Wooden Objects

Pl. 9c.

H81 M22 16: The front part of a sekhem sceptre was found in the debris in the upper burial chamber of Sloping Passage II which belonged to the tomb owner. It is made of one piece of good timber, cut and smoothed to shape. One face of the head of the sceptre shows a longitudinal crack. No traces of colour now remain. Present length: 32.5cm. Widest part of head: 6.5cm.

H81 M22 17: A small part of the tomb owner's staff was found in the upper burial chamber of Sloping Passage II. Present length: 12cm. Diameter: 2.4cm.

Decorated Stone Fragments

Figs. 19, 20.

These limestone fragments were found in the debris which partly filled the chapel and shrine of tomb M22. They are decorated in painting of the same style as that of the wall scenes in the tomb. (F in inventory sequence refers to 'fragment'.)

H81 M22 F1: Two female offering bearers facing left, wearing long wigs, chokers, collars (?), bracelets, anklets (now visible only on the right leg of the second woman) and long, tight dresses with shoulder straps. Each woman supports, with her right hand, an elaborately painted basket carried on her head. The first woman has her left hand by her side, while the second carries a bird.

H81 M22 F2: The face of a female wearing a broad collar, and smelling a lotus flower. This posture may indicate a relationship to the tomb owner.

H81 M22 F3: Part of a broad collar and shoulder straps of a female dress. The dimensions suggest that the fragment belonged to an important figure.

H81 M22 F4: Part of a man's leg.

H81 M22 F5: A man's elbow.

H81 M22 F6: The face and shoulder of a male figure.

H81 M22 F7: The head of a man.

H81 M22 F8: Part of a representation of a male figure carrying a bundle of papyrus. It is likely that this fragment belonged to the east wall of the shrine, where the cutting of papyrus is shown.

H81 M22 F9 – M22 F11: Overlapping legs, showing movements of workmen (?). The large foot in F10, and possibly F9 are difficult to explain in this context.

H81 M22 F12: Part of a male's skirt with the knot at waist.

H81 M22 F13: Two heads of geese.

H81 M22 F14: The representation of a mirror.

H81 M22 F15: Part of frieze decoration, and the sign *smsw* (?).

H81 M22 F16 – M22 F18: Fragments with hieroglyphic signs.

H81 M22 F19 – M22 F20: Not clear.

H81 M22 F21 – M22 F23: Probably parts of frieze (?) decoration.

H81 M22 F24: The letter *n*.

H81 M22 F25: Probably the title *r[ḫ] nswt*.

H81 M22 F26: The name of *Ḥwt-ḥr*.

Pottery

Fig. 21.

H81 M22 01: Bag-shaped jar. Rim broken. Nile silt. Simple wheel made, round base cut and smoothed. Rope impressions near base. Cream slip. H. 17.8cm. D. of rim est. 9cm. BW. 13cm. Th. varies from .8cm. at neck to 2.3cm. at base.

H81 M22 02: Bag-shaped jar. Section of rim missing. Nile silt – well fired. Simple wheel made, round base cut and smoothed. H. 18.9cm. D. of rim undetermined. BW. 14.5cm. Th. varies from .6cm. at neck to 1.6cm. at base.

H81 M22 03: Conical jar. Rim chipped. Nile silt. Hand modelled. Grey slip. Unfired Nile silt moulded into jar, not the remains of a stopper, since it could not be shaken out. H. 29.5cm. D. of rim c. 9.5cm. BW. 13.4cm. Th. varies from 1cm. at rim, base undetermined due to presence of mud.

H81 M22 04: Bag-shaped jar. Rim chipped. Nile silt – well fired. Burn mark on body of jar. Simple wheel made, round base cut and smoothed. H. 20.5cm. D. of rim 9cm. BW. 15.4cm. Th. varies from .7cm. at neck to 2.4cm. at base.

H81 M22 05: Globular jar. Large section of rim missing. Nile silt (very coarse) – unevenly fired, thick black core. Simple wheel made, round base cut and smoothed. Red slip, flaking. H. 18.1cm. D. of rim undetermined. Th. varies from .8cm. at neck to 2cm. at base.

H81 M22 06: Sherd. Section of pot stand. Nile silt – poorly fired, thick black core. Thick red slip. Present height c. 9.2cm. Th. 2cm.

H81 M22 07: Sherd. Section of pot stand. Nile silt – unevenly fired, thick black core. Simple wheel made. Thick red slip on outside and on inside of neck. Present height 22cm. Th. below rim .8cm. and at cut section 1cm.

H81 M22 08: Sherd. Section of pot stand. Nile silt – unevenly fired, thick black core. Simple wheel made. Thick red slip. Present height 27.5cm. D. of rim est. at 12cm. D. of base undetermined. Th. below rim .7cm.

H81 M22 09: Sherd. Section of pot stand. Nile silt – unevenly fired, thick black core. Simple wheel made. Thick red slip. Present height 26cm. Th. near rim .7cm.

H81 M22 10: Sherd. Top section of pot stand. Rim missing. Nile silt – unevenly fired. Thick black core. Thick red slip. Simple wheel made. Body of stand flares out from narrow neck. Present height 18cm. D. of rim undetermined. BW. at base of neck 9.3cm. Th. varies from .3cm. to 1cm.

H81 M22 11: Globular jar. Most of rim missing. Nile silt – well fired. Simple wheel made, round base cut and smoothed. Brown slip. Three bands of rope impressions. Present height c. 19.7cm. D. of rim est. at 10cm. BW. 15.5cm. Th. varies from .6cm. to 2.2cm. at base.

H81 M22 12: Sherd. Base of dish. Nile silt. Simple wheel made, base cut flat. Red slip. Present height 6.5cm. D. of rim undetermined. Th. varies from .7cm. to 1cm.

H81 M22 13: Bag-shaped jar. Rim broken. Nile silt – well fired. Simple wheel made, round base cut and smoothed. H. 19.1cm. D. of rim undetermined. Th. varies from .6cm. to 1.4cm. at base.

H81 M22 14: Bag-shaped jar. Rim broken. Nile silt. Simple wheel made, round base cut and smoothed. Red slip. H. 19.7cm. D. of rim undetermined. BW. 13.1cm. Th. varies from .7cm. at neck to 1.5cm. at base.

H81 M22 15: Globular jar. Rim badly chipped. Nile silt. Simple wheel made, round base cut and smoothed. Red slip inside and out. H. 17.9cm. D. of rim undetermined. BW. 15.1cm. Th. varies from .8cm. to 2.3cm. at base.

NOTES

*Tomb no. 22 in Newberry, *LAAA* 4[1912], 113.

1. For the significance of this title see Martin-Pardey, *Provinzialverwaltung,* 94ff.
2. Ibid, 96ff.
3. For the reading and interpretation of this title see Brunner, *SAK* 1[1974], 58f.; Fischer, *Varia*, 8, n.15.
4. Ranke, *Personennamen* 1, 327:7.
5. Borchardt, *Denkmäler*, CG 1585.
6. Ranke, *Personennamen* 1, 41:3. This is the only example of the name given by Ranke.
7. *LAAA* 4[1912], 113. It appears that he wrongly combines the titles *ḥmt-nṯr Ḥwt-ḥr nbt nht* and *ḥmt-nṯr Ḥqt* on the false door. His questioning whether the holder of the two titles was the tomb owner's mother is not justified. The seated figure after the word *nht* on the false door refers most probably to the name *Špsjt* [*-k3w*], whom he identifies as the wife.
8. *Personennamen* 1, 171:12.
9. Ibid, 183:27.
10. Ibid, 215:1.
11. Ibid, 68:6.
12. For names formed with *Q3j* + the name of a god see ibid, 332. But *Q3j-Mnw* is not listed there.
13. *El-Hawawish* 3, 10.
14. Reisner, *Giza Necropolis* 1, 241, 246, 256ff. See rock tombs type RC (IV), and mastaba chapels type (5).
15. For examples of rock cut tombs see Rachewiltz, *Irw-K3-Ptḥ,* fig. 1, pl. 1; Moussa-Junge, *Two Tombs*, 18, fig. 1. For mastabas see Mariette, *Mastabas*, 115, 159, 196, 222, 285, 330.
16. Brunner, *Felsgräber*, figs. 4, 5. See also the earlier tombs at Tehna, ibid, figs. 2, 3.
17. *El-Hawawish* 3, 11.
18. Ibid.
19. Mackay, *Hemamieh,* pls. 19, 20, 27, 28; Smith, *HESPOK*, 216.
20. Ibid, 215.
21. See e.g. Rachewiltz, *Irw-K3-Ptḥ*, pls. 4ff.
22. Fifth Dynasty mastabas had statues, of course, but placed in a serdab. This seems also to be the case at Deshasha, where statues of Nen-Khefet-ka and his similarly named son were found (Petrie, *Deshasheh*, pls. 30-32).
23. For comparison see Smith, *HESPOK*, 193-94, 201, 216.
24. Fischer, *Varia*, 4. We should note that chairs with bulls' legs reappeared in the Middle Kingdom (Vandier, *Manuel* 4, 84).
25. See for example Davies, *Sheikh Saïd*, pls. 4, 9, 20, 29, 31; Mackay, *Hemamieh*, pls. 12, 16, 22, 27, 28; Épron-Wild, *Ti*, pls. 149, 161, 172; Petrie-Murray, *Tomb Chapels*, pls. 3, 11; Moussa-Altenmüller, *Nefer*, pls. 24, 38; id., *Nianchchnum*, figs. 4, 11, 20, 26. At Sheikh Said the use of bulls'

legs appears to have continued in Dynasty 6.

26. Schäfer, *Principles*, 40.
27. For example, Lepsius, *Denkmäler* II, 53, 57; Junker, *Gîza* 3, fig. 21; vol. 6, fig. 13; vol. 7, fig. 71; Badawy, *Iteti*, fig. 27; Brunner-Traut, *Seschemnofers III*, fig. 4; Simpson, *Kawab*, fig. 49; id., *Western Cemetery* 1, figs. 6, 7, 32. See also James, *Hieroglyphic Texts*, pl. 12, where the flower is presented by the tomb owner's wife.
28. Moussa-Altenmüller, *Nianchchnum*, pl. 69, fig. 25.
29. Ibid, 44-45.
30. Ibid, 58, fig. 5.
31. Lepsius, *Denkmäler* II, 60; De Morgan, *Dahchour* 2, pl. 24; Junker, *Gîza* 4, fig. 8a; Vandier, *Manuel* 4, 724, fig. 299; Moussa-Junge, *Two Tombs*, pl. 12; Moussa-Altenmüller, *Nianchchnum*, pl. 4, fig. 5.
32. Davies, *Ptahhetep* 1, pl. 22; Junker, *Gîza* 11, fig. 63.
33. Vandier, *Manuel* 4, 718.
34. Épron-Wild, *Ti*, pls. 156-57, 159, 164; Moussa-Altenmüller, *Nefer*, pl. 1ff.; Moussa-Junge, *Two Tombs*, pl. 12; Moussa-Altenmüller, *Nianchchnum*, fig. 4ff.
35. Fischer, *Dendera*, 81-82; *El-Hawawish* 1, fig. 14; vol. 2, fig. 26; vol. 3, fig. 9.
36. Davies, *Ptahhetep* 1, pl. 18, no. 409.
37. Épron-Wild, *Ti*, pls. 170, 186.
38. Rusch, *ZÄS* 58 [1923], 107-108, pl. A.
39. For a recent study of this problem see Wiebach, *Scheintür*, 9-10, 128ff.
40. *LAAA* 4 [1912], 113.
41. *Dendera*, 11, n. 51, 69-70.
42. *LAAA* 4 [1912], 114. See now *El-Hawawish* 1, 9ff. The tomb has not yet been allocated a number in our complete survey of the mountain.
43. Gomaà, *Ersten Zwischenzeit*, 83, n. 7.
44. This is Newberry's tomb no. 25 (*LAAA* 4 [1912], 115), which he dates to Dynasty 12. As work progresses in this tomb a much earlier date seems more likely.
45. Compare with Ka-khent and his son (?) Ka-khent of Hemamia, where this same office appears to have passed from father to son (Mackay, *Hemamieh*, pls. 22, 12).
46. Baer, *Rank and Title*, 231-32.
47. For the identification of the similarly-named father and son, Ka-khent, see Baer, ibid, 147-48, no. [543].
48. For Ka-khent's wife see Mackay, *Hemamieh*, pl. 22.
49. Because of the damaged state of his tomb, Hesi-Min's titles are, of course, incomplete. Like Ka-khent, he might have been *jmj-r wpt* 'overseer of commissions' (Mackay, *Hemamieh*, pls. 21ff.). This title appears with his son (?) Min-ankh (*El-Hawawish* 1, fig. 4).
50. Mackay, *Hemamieh*, pl. 20.
51. Ibid, pls. 23, 24.
52. Kanawati, *Governmental Reforms*, 1-12.
53. This is the figure established upon completion of the survey of square M. An approximate figure of 200 metres above mean sea level was given to M8 in *El-Hawawish* 3, 14.
54. *LAAA* 4 [1912], 113.
55. The sign  is presumably an error for  *šs*.
56. Compare with Fischer, *Varia*, 6, fig. 3, where the two ewers face in opposite directions towards the man and his wife sitting opposite each other at an offering table.
57. *nb* may be confidently restored after the similar inscriptions on the adjacent west wall of the chapel, and on the north wall of the shrine.
58. For example, Lepsius, *Denkmäler* II, 53, 57; Junker, *Gîza* 3, fig. 21; vol. 7, fig. 71; Brunner-Traut, *Seschemnofers III*, fig. 4.
59. Junker, *Giza* 6, fig. 13; Badawy, *Iteti*, fig. 27.
60. In the tomb of *Jzj* at Deir el-Gebrawi, there appears to be more than one flower presented. But the scene there is fragmentary and one cannot be certain that it belongs to the same theme, for it seems that the lotus flowers were carried together with other offerings by the same man (Davies, *Deir el-Gebrâwi* 2, pl. 20). Compare with the first offering bearer in the tomb of *Ṯjj* (Épron-Wild, *Ti*, pl. 161).

61. The same comment was made by Badawy, *Iteti*, 27.
62. For another example of flowers not received possibly because the tomb owner holds something in his hands see Davies, *Deir, el-Gebrâwi* 2, pl. 20.
63. Lepsius, *Denkmäler* II, 53; possibly Junker, *Gîza* 3, fig. 21; Badawy, *Iteti*, 27; Brunner-Traut, *Seschemnofers III*, fig. 4.
64. See for example, Davies, *Sheikh Saïd*, pls. 4, 9; Junker, *Gîza* 3, fig. 13; Blackman, *Meir* 4, pl. 11; Épron-Wild, *Ti*, pls. 161-62.
65. For similar decoration see, Moussa-Altenmüller, *Nianchchnum*, pl. 69, fig. 25.
66. On these technical points see, Hickmann, *ASAE* 48 [1948], 639ff.; Vandier, *Manuel* 4, 365.
67. Montet, *Vie privée*, 361.
68. Badawy, *Iteti*, 27, translates as 'ox of the meadows'.
69. See also Davies, *Ptahhetep*, pl. 21; Hassan, *Giza* 6-part 3, fig. 98; Duell, *Mereruka*, pl. 51; Vandier, *Manuel* 5, fig. 18, no. 5.
70. This appears to be the second scribal error on this wall, the first being the writing of  for  above the offering table (see n. 55 above).
71. Montet, *Vie privée*, 97; Vandier, *Manuel* 5, 58.
72. *El-Hawawish* 1, fig. 10; vol. 2, fig. 20.
73. I am grateful to Dr. H. G. Fischer and Dr. K. A. Kitchen for valuable suggestions on the translation of this text.
74. Vandier, *Manuel* 4, 796-97, figs. 446, 449; and Davies, *Ptahhetep* 1, pl. 22; Junker, *Gîza* 11, fig. 63.
75. Vandier, *Manuel* 4, 720ff. For a spear held at an even greater angle, 30°, see Moussa-Altenmüller, *Nianchchnum*, pl. 4, fig. 5.
76. For imitations of reeds, but in staves, see Fischer, *MMJ* 13 [1978], 21.
77. For similar arrangement see Davies, *Deir el-Gebrâwi* 1, pl. 3; vol. 2, pls. 5, 23; and probably Petrie, *Deshasheh*, pl. 24.
78. The same may be observed in Petrie, *Deshasheh*, pl. 22.
79. For the interpretation of this 'mountain of water' see Junker, *Gîza* 4, 28ff.; Mohr, *Hetep-her-akhti*, 69-70; Vandier, *Manuel* 4, 731-33.
80. Fragments of the *k3* signs, painted in brown colour, are clearly visible.
81. Servin, *ASAE* 48 [1948], 66-67; Davies, *Deir el-Gebrâwi* 1, pls. 3, 5; Blackman, *Meir* 4, pl. 7; vol. 5, pl. 24; Moussa-Altenmüller, *Nianchchnum*, pl. 4, fig. 5.
82. Davies, *Deir el-Gebrâwi* 2, pl. 3.
83. Lepsius, *Denkmäler* II, 60; Davies, *Deir el-Gebrâwi* 2, pl. 5; Blackman, *Meir* 4, pl. 7; Duell, *Mereruka*, pls. 9-13; Junker, *Gîza* 4, fig. 8; vol. 11, fig. 60.
84. Lepsius, *Denkmäler* II, 60; Duell, *Mereruka*, pls. 9-13; Junker, *Gîza* 11, fig. 60.
85. For a single fisherman in a boat see Davies, *Ptahhetep* 2, pl. 13; Mohr, *Hetep-her-akhti*, fig. 34; Junker, *Gîza* 11, fig. 60; Épron-Wild, *Ti*, pl. 117; Moussa-Altenmüller, *Nianchchnum*, fig. 12.
86. For the identification of the different types of fish see Gamer-Wallert, *Fische*, pls. 1-6.
87. Vandier, *Manuel* 5, 536.
88. It is important to notice that a club is also represented in the tomb of Kheni (*El-Hawawish* 2, fig, 22), and possibly in the tomb of Ka-hep (ibid 1, fig. 12). Both tombs were decorated by the same artist, Seni.
89. The same appears in Davies, *Deir el-Gebrâwi* 2, pl. 5; Blackman, *Meir* 5, pls. 24, 28; Moussa-Altenmüller, *Nianchchnum*, pl. 4, fig. 5.
90. See n. 86 above.
91. As, e.g., in Petrie, *Deshasheh*, pl. 22; Blackman, *Meir* 4, pl. 7; Épron-Wild, *Ti*, pl. 117.
92. As in Davies, *Sheikh Saïd*, pl. 11; Varille, *Ni-ankh-Pepi*, fig, 4; Saleh, *Tombs at Thebes*, pl. 19; *El-Hawawish* 2, fig. 18.
93. As, e.g., in Blackman, *Meir* 5, pl. 24.
94. See n. 86 above.
95. See Blackman, *Meir* 5, pls. 15, 32; *El-Hawawish* 1, fig. 9.
96. Compare with other 'punishment' scenes, e.g., in Davies, *Deir el-Gebrâwi* 1, pl. 8; Épron-Wild, *Ti*, pl. 168; Dunham-Simpson, *Mersyankh III*, fig. 9.
97. For references to this relatively common attitude see Vandier, *Manuel* 5, 36.

98. For the meaning of *pr-ḏt* see Menu-Harari, *CRIPEL* 2 [1974], 142ff.
99. For similar inscriptions see Montet, *Vie privée*, 147-48. I take the plural genitive *nw* to refer to the *jmjw-r ṯzwt*. For a holder of the title *jmj-r ṯzt n pr-ḏt* see Davies, *Deir el-Gebrâwi* 2, pl. 4.
100. Compare, e.g., with Épron-Wild, *Ti*, pl. 173; *El-Hawawish* 2, fig. 19.
101. Davies, *Sheikh Saïd*, pl. 4; Épron-Wild, *Ti*, pl. 173; *El-Hawawish* 1, fig. 9; vol. 2, fig. 19.
102. The same is depicted in the tomb of Ibi of Deir el-Gebrawi (Davies, *Deir el-Gebrâwi* 1, pl. 14) and Ka-hep (*El-Hawawish* 1, fig. 9). For workmen holding the round stones see Drenkhahn, *Handwerker*, fig. 13; Épron-Wild, *Ti*, pl. 173.
103. Montet, *Vie privée*, 284; Drenkhahn, *Handwerker*, 20-21.
104. Lepsius, *Denkmäler* II, 19, 23; Junker, *Gîza* 3, fig. 27; Brunner-Traut, *Seschemnofers III*, fig. 3.
105. For other examples of two false doors of different sizes placed in the west wall see, Lepsius, *Denkmäler* II, 19; Brunner-Traut, *Seschemnofers III*, fig. 3; James, *Hieroglyphic Texts*, pl. 28.
106. A similar arrangement occurs in the neighbouring tomb, M23 (to be published), where each of the two jambs appears to be designed as a complete false door.
107. Vandier, *Manuel* 2, 398.
108. Ibid, 400.
109. Ibid, 422.
110. Ibid, 414.
111. Ibid, 427.
112. Ibid, 411.
113. The letter  was originally written in outline, but was left out in the final colouring.
114. Brunner-Traut, *Seschemnofers III*, pl. 21, fig. 3.
115. Newberry's copy (*LAAA* 4 [1912], 113) seems to add a priesthood of Heket in this place. There is no trace of this title now on the false door, nor is it likely to have existed. Note also that the order of signs in Newberry's copy is confused.
116. The sign for *Mnw* would, of course, be placed at the beginning of the name as a result of honorific transposition.
117. The staff after *z3.f* is almost certainly part of the sign *smsw*.
118. Compare with the similar inscriptions on the south and west walls of the chapel.
119. For the various postures of workmen see Vandier, *Manuel* 5, 498ff.
120. Petrie, *Deshasheh*, pl. 5; Davies, *Sheikh Saïd*, pl. 12; Mohr, *Hetep-her-akhti*, 58, fig. 27.
121. The verb means 'calfater' according to Montet (*Vie privée*, 79) and 'tasser et lier' or 'construire' according to Servin, *ASAE* 48 [1948], 82ff.
122. Similar scenes are usually labelled *spt smḥ* 'constructing a boat', or *spt smḥ m mḥt* 'constructing a boat in the marshland', etc. (Montet, *Vie privée*, 79). The word *smḥ* 'boat' seems unlikely in our case. There is no space for the *s*, and the *t* after *mḥ* (?) is clear.
123. This appears to be a shortened form of *spt smḥ m mḥt* as in Davies, *Ptahhetep* 2, pl. 13.
124. It could also mean 'beating' the flax: Edel, *Grammatik*, § 62.
125. For *ṯ3t* see Montet, *Vie privée*, 198, 233.
126. This is following Simpson, *Western Cemetery*, 2, fig. 4. Montet, *Vie privée*, 233, prefers to render it as 'extraire les graines de lin'.
127. For similar inscriptions see Montet, *Vie privée*, 69-72. The closest to our text is his inscription no. 9, after Lepsius, *Denkmäler* II, 105.
128. The expression 'may your hand endure upon the water', was later repeated twice in tombs at this cemetery (*El-Hawawish* 1, fig. 12; vol. 2, fig. 22).
129. The animal processions in the tombs of Ka-hep (*El-Hawawish* 1, fig. 14) and Kheni (ibid 2, fig. 26) are also depicted on the east wall, facing north, towards the interior of the shrine.
130. Compare with *El-Hawawish* 2, fig. 19.
131. For mummies where plaster was used in the Old Kingdom see Smith, *HESPOK*, 27-28; Moussa-Altenmüller, *Nefer*, 43, pl. 40.

THE TOMB OF KHENI-ANKHU

H 15*

I THE TOMB OWNER AND HIS DEPENDANT

The Tomb Owner

NAME

Hnj-ᶜnḫw 'Kheni-ankhu'. The name is not listed in Ranke, *Personennamen.*

TITLES

1 – *jmj-r ḥm-nṯr* 'overseer of priests'.
2 – *jmj-r Šmᶜ m3ᶜ* 'true overseer of Upper Egypt'.(1)
3 – *jrj-pᶜt* 'hereditary prince'.
4 – *ḥ3tj-ᶜ* 'count'.
5 – *ḥrj-ḥbt* 'lector priest'.
6 – *sm3 Mnw* 'stolist of Min'.

Dependant

The man represented before the tomb owner may well be his son. Above him the sign *ṯ3* stands at the beginning of a damaged inscription, and is probably part of his name.(2) Many names begin with *ṯ3*,(3) but one of the strong possibilities is *Ṯ3wtj*, which was a popular name towards the end of the Old Kingdom and in the First Intermediate Period, particularly in the neighbouring nomes 5-7.(4) A man named *Ṯ3wtj-jqr* who possessed the titles *jt-nṯr mrjj-nṯr jrj-pᶜt ḥ3tj-ᶜ ḥrj-ḥbt smr wᶜtj jmj-r Šmᶜ jmj-r ḥm-nṯr sm3 Mnw*, left inscriptions at Wadi Hammamat.(5) Because of the priesthood of Min in *Ṯ3wtj-jqr's* titles, Kees has correctly suggested that he could have been either from Akhmim or Coptos, the two centres for the cult of this god.(6) But since the name is not attested at Akhmim the preference has been to associate him with nome 5.(7) It should be noticed, however, that although the viziers *Šm3j*(8) and his son *Jdj* of Coptos(9) were priests of Min, neither of the two overseers of Upper Egypt at Coptos, *Wsr* and *Ṯ3wtj*,(10) who were not viziers, is known to have held this priesthood, which was, on the other hand, particularly common at Akhmim. Since *Ṯ3wtj-jqr* of Wadi Hammamat bears the same titles as those of *Hnj-ᶜnḫw* of Akhmim, and since the latter's son is likely to have been named *Ṯ3wtj*, the identification of *Ṯ3wtj-jqr* with *Hnj-ᶜnḫw's* son should be seriously considered. The fact that the inscriptions at Wadi Hammamat add the word *jqr* after *Ṯ3wtj's* name, and *jt-nṯr mrjj-nṯr* in his titulary, should not argue against his possible identification with the Akhmim official. The epithet *jqr* was used earlier at Akhmim by *Ṯtj-jqr*,(11) probably of the same family of *Hnj-ᶜnḫw*, and the titles *jt-nṯr mrjj-nṯr* are also attested at Akhmim in the case of *Ḥrwj*,(12) who was perhaps a contemporary.(13)

II DATING OF KHENI-ANKHU

1 – The tomb is situated to the east of that of Shepsi-pu-min (H24), at a slightly higher level. It is also immediately next to H14, a tomb with a portico supported by two pillars, which is similar to H24 and H26 and could not have been much removed from them in time. The last two tombs are dated to the end of Dynasty 6,(14) and the higher level, as already discussed under M22, probably indicates a later date.

2 – The name of the tomb owner is similar to one of Shepsi-pu-Min's (H24) names.(15)

3. – The writing of *ḥ3tj-ᶜ* at the end of the sequence of titles and just before the name may point to a date after the Old Kingdom.(16)

These points, together with the inferior quality of art suggest a date in the Eighth Dynasty or during the Heracleopolitan Period.

III ARCHITECTURAL FEATURES

Figs. 22 – 24.

The tomb is excavated in the south-west face of the mountain at a height of 230 metres above the mean sea level, i.e. only 5 metres above that of *Špsj-pw-Mnw* (H24). The quality of the rock in this area of the mountain is good and smooth surfaces can be obtained, yet most of the walls were left in an incomplete and rough condition.

The Forecourt

By cutting back the face of the cliff in order to create a facade for the tomb, a forecourt, 4.00m. E-W x 6.00m. N-S, was formed with two distinctly defined side walls sloping from the height of the façade to the floor of the forecourt, which is largely uneven as a result of massive pieces of rock left uncut. The façade, well cut on a sloping line, measures 4.65m. wide and 3.15m. in height from the top of a well defined and complete lintel, .30m. high, extending the entire width of the façade. One complete and two incomplete burial pits are excavated in the forecourt area.

The Chapel

An irregular sloping path from the forecourt leads down to the entrance in the centre of the façade, ending in one shallow step, .10m. high, which gives access to the floor of the doorway. The doorway to the chapel measures 1.00m. wide, 2.40m. high from below the drum, and tapers upwards in thickness from 1.35m. at the floor to .95m. just below the drum. Internally, the doorway is defined by an internal door recess. From the doorway two shallow steps, one .10m. high and the other .15m. high, lead to the floor of the chapel.

The incomplete chapel appears to have been planned as rectangular in shape with a row of pillars in an E-W axis (see the tombs of *Ṯtj-jqr* and *Špsj-pw-Mnw*),[17] but the project was clearly abandoned at an early stage. The present E-W length of the chapel is 7.80m., but the width varies considerably depending on the degree of progress of the cutting in the area. The sloping ceiling reaches a height of 3.10m. opposite the entrance, but is much less in the eastern part of the chapel as a result of the floor level being higher with a large amount of rock left uncut. The tomb as it stands has two pillars, and a possible third one just begun, surmounted by an architrave. Only the central pillar progressed far enough to have three of its four sides free, still being attached to the mother rock at the back. The south face of this pillar is the only place in the tomb which received plaster and decoration. The pillars and the architrave both slope towards the north; similarly the ceiling has an upward inclination from the entrance wall. An unusual feature of this tomb is that most of the walls, the sides of the pillars, and the walls of the shafts are sloping and not vertical. The unfinished state of this tomb presents valuable information on the order of stages in excavating a tomb.

IV BURIAL APARTMENTS

Figs. 22 – 24.

Inside the Chapel

One vertical and two sloping passages, all found plundered, are excavated in the floor of the chapel.

I To the left of the doorway and parallel to the entrance wall is a vertical, rectangular shaft which measures 2.10m. x .85m. x 2.55m. deep. At floor level opens a well cut rectangular burial recess into the south wall. This measures 2.30m. x .70m. x .90m. high, and has a sloping ceiling.

II Perpendicular to the entrance wall and between the two pillars is a sloping passage, well cut into good rock. Its mouth measures 2.10m. average length x 1.00m. in width.

The passage descends in one slope at an angle of 35° for a length of 5.00m. At the beginning of the passage, its sides are tapered upwards, and the entrance is defined and decorated by two projecting narrow jambs having the same height as the passage, 1.35m. At the bottom of the slope is a depression .55m. deep beyond which lies a horizontal corridor that curves slightly to the right in its second half. This passage is 5.80m. long x .90m. wide x 1.10m. high, and terminates in a burial chamber cut at an angle to the right. The burial chamber is of irregular shape with soft corners, having a maximum length of 2.85m., a maximum width of 2.30m. and a height of 1.25m.

III A second sloping passage lies to the right of the central pillar and is axial with the doorway. Its mouth measures 2.10m. x 1.05m. and its sides taper upwards. The passage descends at an angle of 30° for a length of 7.50m., then changes to a 10° angle for a further 1.40m. The burial chamber has curved walls and is irregular in shape, with a maximum length of 3.20m., a maximum width of 1.95m. and an average height of 1.05m. Unlike Sloping Passage II, which is cut in fine quality rock, this passage and its chamber are excavated in rock of very poor quality, with the result that all its surfaces are rough in shape and finish, and both walls and ceiling are broken in many places.

Outside the Chapel

One complete and two incomplete burial apartments are excavated in the forecourt area. All were found plundered.

(a) Adjacent to the western wall of the forecourt is a small, unevenly cut and incomplete pit measuring 1.25m. x .75m. and which is excavated to a depth of only .60m.

(b) An almost vertical (80°) pit is cut on an E-W orientation contiguous with the left side of the façade. This well cut pit measures 1.80m. x .85m. x 1.65m. deep. Above the mouth and cut into the sloping western wall of the forecourt is a niche which contains an offering ledge. The outline of this niche is cut on a sloping line (similar to that of the entrance doorway). The niche measures 1.15m. wide, .80m. high and .50m. deep. Originally it was completely plastered and decorated, but only one small fragment remains of light brown plaster with white paint. The floor of the shaft is 2.30m. x .75m. Into the south wall at floor level is cut a large rectangular burial chamber with a low sloping ceiling. It measures 2.30m. x 1.50m., with a height of .85m. at the entrance and .70m. at the south wall.

(c) Adjacent and parallel to the eastern wall of the forecourt is an incomplete sloping pit with a mouth 1.75m. x .75m. and an unfinished depth of 1.05m., being cut in what appears to be two different inclines. The entrance is decorated with a sloping line cut to represent a narrow jamb. Above the pit and cut into the sloping eastern wall of the forecourt is a small and incomplete niche, which has a lintel but is irregular in the lower part. The niche measures .85m. high x .60m. wide x .15m. deep; the lintel has the same width as the niche and a depth of .10m.

V SCENES AND INSCRIPTIONS

Fig. 25.

The only part of the tomb which received plaster and decoration in painting is the south face of the central pillar. The rest of the surfaces are unplastered; in fact the cutting of the tomb itself was never completed.

The tomb owner stands facing right towards his burial chamber (sloping passage III). He wears a shoulder-length wig, a broad collar over a diagonal sash, bracelets, a short skirt and the leopard skin, of which only a part is now visible, including the tail. He also holds the long staff with the left hand.

Three horizontal lines of hieroglyphs above the tomb owner's figure read: (1) *ḥtp dj nswt Wsjr nb Ḏdw*[18] *prt-ḫrw [n] jrj-[p]ᶜt* (2) *jmj-r Šmᶜ m3ᶜ ḫrj-ḥbt sm3 Mnw jmr-r ḥm-nṯr ḥ3tj-ᶜ* (3) *Ḫnj-ᶜnḫw* '(1) An offering which the king gives and Osiris, lord of Busiris (gives). May an invocation offering come forth for the hereditary prince, (2) the true overseer of Upper Egypt, the lector priest, the stolist of Min, the overseer of priests, the count, (3) Kheni-ankhu'. In front of him is repeated: *ḥ3tj-ᶜ Ḫnj-ᶜnḫw* 'the count, Kheni-ankhu'.

Between his figure and the long staff held with his left hand appears a small figure of a man wearing a short, pointed skirt, his arms at his side. Above him only one sign remains, *ṯ3*, probably representing the initial sign of his name – *Ṯ3wtj* (?).

VI FINDS

Figs. 26, 27.

H81 H15 01: Globular jar. Nile silt – red – well fired. Top wheel turned, round base cut and smoothed. Three rows of rope impressions around body. H. 18cm. BW. 16.3cm. Th. varies from 1cm. at neck to 1.3cm. at base.

H81 H15 02: Sherd. Part of body, neck and rim of vessel. Nile silt – red – unevenly fired, grey core. Present height 9.1cm. D. of rim 9cm. Th. at neck .7cm.

H81 H15 03: Incomplete globular jar. Nile silt – red – unevenly fired. Top wheel turned, round base cut and smoothed. Present height 15.5cm. D. of rim undetermined. BW. 12.9cm. Th. varies from .8cm. at neck to 1.5cm. at base.

H81 H15 04: Sherd. Lower part of vessel. Nile silt – red – unevenly fired, black core. Base cut and smoothed. Present height 10cm. BW. 15.6cm. Th. varies from .6cm. to 1.5cm.

H81 H15 05: Bag shaped jar. Marl clay – coarse. Top wheel turned, round base roughly moulded. H.16.5cm. Estimated D. of rim 9cm. BW. 11.4cm. Th. varies from 1cm. to 2.8cm. at base.

H81 H15 06: Globular jar. Nile silt – red – unevenly fired, buff core. Top wheel turned, round base cut and smoothed. H. 16.9cm. Estimated D. of rim 9cm. BW. 15.5cm. Th. varies from .3cm. at neck to 1.9cm. at base.

H81 H15 07: Globular jar. Nile silt – black inside and out – red core, unevenly fired. Top wheel turned, round base cut and smoothed. Cream slip on outside. H. 19.6cm. Estimated D. of rim 10cm. BW. 17.6cm. Th. varies from .7cm. at neck to 1cm. at base.

H81 H15 08: Lower section of conical jar. Nile silt – red with black core, unevenly fired. Hand moulded with uneven surface. Present height 16.5cm. BW. 11.4cm. Th. varies from 1.1cm. to 1.8cm. at base.

H81 H15 09: Incomplete globular jar. Nile silt – red – well fired. Top wheel turned, round base cut and smoothed. Present height 16cm. D. of rim undetermined. BW. 14.1cm. Th. varies from .7cm. to 1.9cm. at base.

H81 H15 10: Globular jar. Marl clay – pink – well fired. Top wheel turned, round base cut and smoothed. Buff slip. H. 17.9cm. Estimated D. of rim 10cm. BW. 14.9cm. Th. varies from .5cm. at neck to 1.5cm. at base.

H81 H15 11: Incomplete globular jar. Nile silt – red – unevenly fired, buff core. Top wheel turned, round base cut and smoothed. String impression around body. Present height 16cm. D. of rim undetermined. BW. 14cm. Th. varies from .6cm. at neck to 1.3cm. at base.

H81 H15 12: Incomplete globular jar. Nile silt – red – well fired. Top wheel turned, round base cut and smoothed. Present height 14.4cm. D. of rim undetermined. BW. 12.2cm. Th. varies from .9cm. to 1.7cm. at base.

H81 H15 13: Incomplete globular jar. Nile silt – red – well fired. Top wheel turned, round base cut and smoothed. Buff slip. Present height 18.5 cm. D. of rim undetermined. BW. 14 cm. Th. varies from .4 cm. at neck to 2.7 cm. at base.

H81 H15 14: Globular jar. Marl clay – buff coloured – unevenly fired, red core. Top wheel turned, round base cut and smoothed. H. 19.5 cm. Estimated D. of rim 10 cm. BW. 15.2 cm. Th. varies from .6 cm. at neck to 1.2 cm. at base.

H81 H15 15: Bowl. Marl clay. Wheel turned. Thick red slip inside and outside, polished. H. 5.3 cm. D. 11.7 cm. Th. .9 cm.

H81 H15 16: Bowl. Marl clay – buff – unevenly fired. Wheel turned with roughly cut flat base. H. 5.3 cm. D. of rim 15 cm. D. of base 8 cm. Th. varies from .8 cm. to 1.1 cm.

H81 H15 17: Bowl, Nile silt – red – unevenly fired, buff core. Wheel turned, roughly cut flat base. H. 6.3 cm. D. of rim 15 cm. D. of base 6 cm.

H81 H15 18: Globular jar. Nile silt – red – badly fired, grey core. Top wheel turned, round base cut and smoothed. Buff slip H. 17.8 cm. D. of rim 12 cm. BW. 15.5 cm. Th. varies from .5 cm. at neck to 1.7 cm. at base.

H81 H15 19: Globular jar. Nile silt – red – unevenly fired, grey/black core. Top wheel turned, round base cut and smoothed. H. 16.5 cm. D. of rim 8.2 cm. BW. 14 cm. Th. varies from .6 cm. at neck to 1.9 cm. at base.

H81 H15 20: Globular jar. Nile silt – red – unevenly fired, grey core. Top wheel turned, round base cut and smoothed. White slip. H. 16 cm. D. of rim 8 cm. BW. 13.4 cm. Th. varies from .7 cm. at neck to 2.6 cm. at base.

H81 H15 21: Globular jar. Nile silt – red – unevenly fired, grey core. Top wheel turned, round base cut and smoothed. Buff slip. H. 15.9 cm. D. of rim 10 cm. BW. 14.4 cm. Th. varies from .7 cm. at neck to 1.7 cm. at base.

H81 H15 22: Bag shaped jar. Nile silt – red – unevenly fired. Top wheel turned, round base cut and smoothed. Buff slip. H. 17 cm. D. of rim undetermined. BW. 12.4 cm. Th. varies from 1 cm. at neck to 2.7 cm. at base.

H81 H15 23: Globular jar. Marl clay – evenly fired. Top wheel turned, round base cut and smoothed. Buff colour. H. 18 cm. D. of rim 10 cm. BW. 14.6 cm. Th. varies from .6 cm. at shoulder to 2.1 cm. at base.

H81 H15 24: Globular jar. Nile silt – red – unevenly fired, buff core. Top wheel turned, round base cut and smoothed. Rope impressions around lower part of body. H. 15 cm. D. of rim 8 cm. Th. varies from .6 cm. at neck to 1.2 cm. at lower part of body to .8 cm. at base.

H81 H15 25: Globular jar. Mixture of Nile silt and Marl clay, patchy, red, pink, buff, grey, unevenly fired, grey/black core. Top wheel turned, round base cut and smoothed. H. 16.7 cm. D. of rim 8.2 cm. BW. 13.4 cm. Th. varies from .6 cm. to 2 cm. at base.

H81 H15 26: Incomplete globular jar. Nile silt – red – well fired. Top wheel turned, round base cut roughly, flat area not centred. Buff slip. H. estimated at 15.4 cm. D. of rim undetermined. BW. 12.2 cm. Th. varies from .8 cm. at neck to 2.1 cm. at base.

H81 H15 27: Globular jar. Nile silt – patchy red/buff – well fired, thin grey/brown core. Top wheel turned, round base cut and smoothed. Buff slip. Blackened inside and outside. H. 21.3 cm. D. of rim 10 cm. BW. 17.8 cm. Th. varies from .9 cm. at neck to 2.4 cm. at base.

H81 H15 28: Globular jar. Nile silt – red – well fired. Top wheel turned, round base cut and smoothed. Buff slip. H. 15.8 cm. D. of rim 9 cm. BW. 12.8 cm. Th. varies from .8 cm. at neck to 2 cm. at base.

H81 H15 29: Globular jar, large storage jar. Marl clay – pink – well fired. Top wheel turned, round base cut and smoothed. H. 30cm. D. of rim 10.5cm. BW. 28cm. Th. varies from 1cm. at neck to 1.3cm. on body to 2cm. at base.

NOTES

*Tomb no. 10 in Newberry, *LAAA* 4[1912], 107.

1. For other holders of this title see *Wnj* (Sethe, *Urk.* 1, 110:2; Fischer, *Varia,* pl. 20); *Ṯ3wtj* of Qasr el-Saiyad (Montet, *Kemi* 6 [1936], 100); *jbj* and *Ḏꜥw* of Deir el-Gebrawi (Davies, *Deir el-Gebrâwi* 1, pl. 23; vol. 2, pls. 6,7); *N-ꜥnḫ-Ppjj, Ppjj-ꜥnḫ/Ḥnjj-km* and *Ppjj-ꜥnḫ ḥrj-jb* of Meir (Blackman, Meir 5, pls. 14, 25, 28, 34). Both *Ppjj-ꜥnḫ-ḥrj-jb* of Meir (ibid 4, pls. 6:1, 15), and *Jdw* I of Dendera (Fischer, *Dendera,* 93), were described as *jmj-r Šmꜥ n bw m3ꜥ;* but *ꜥb-jḥw,* also of Dendera, was *jmj-r Šmꜥ m3ꜥ* (ibid, 195, fig. 40).
2. The sign is clearly *ṯ3* and not, for example, *z3.*
3. *Ranke, Personennamen* 1, 386ff.
4. See Fischer, *Coptite Nome,* pl. 14; Fischer, *Dendera,* 103ff., 175f.; Montet, *Kemi* 6[1936], 87ff.
5. Couyat-Montet, *Hammamat,* 90ff., pl. 35; Sethe, *Urk.* 1,258: 14-15, 259:7-8, 259:17.
6. 'Provinzialverwaltung', NGWG [1932], 110.
7. Gomaà, *Ersten Zwischenzeit,* 50; Martin-Pardey, *Provinzialverwaltung,* 223, 227; Kanawati, *Governmental Reforms,* 118.
8. Goedicke, *Königliche Dokumente,* Figs. 18, 23, 27.
9. Ibid, fig. 28.
10. Fischer, *Coptite Nome,* pls. 13, 14.
11. *El-Hawawish* 1, 12ff.
12. Newberry, LAAA 4 [1912], 105.
13. Kanawati, *Governmental Reforms,* 120.
14. *El-Hawawish* 1, 13-14; vol. 2, 11-14.
15. Ibid 2, 7.
16. Helck, *Verwaltung,* 207.
17. *El-Hawawish* 1, fig. 5; vol. 2, fig. 1.
18. Notice the writing of the *d* before the *ḏd.*

THE STELA OF SHEPSIT-KAU

CG 1585

Pl. 10; Fig. 28.

This stela, which came from Akhmim, is now in the Cairo Museum. A brief description of its scenes and a transcription of its text have been published in Borchardt, *Denkmäler*, but without a photograph or line drawing. The limestone stela is now broken in many parts around the edges, its present width being .43m. and height .33m. (maximum). The work on the stela was certainly left incomplete, with many lines and some hieroglyphic signs before the owner's face marked only in black ink. The projecting piece of stone in the top right corner appears, however, to have been left deliberately uncut, perhaps as a result of a flaw in the stone, since the *ḥtp dj nswt* formula, in the first line of text, starts to the left of the projection and the signs in the second line are cut into this same faulty area. The hieroglyphic signs, except for those in front of Shepsit-kau's face which are written in black ink, are all incised. The scenes are executed in sunk relief, with the modelling of figures roughly finished.

The owner of the stela, facing right, sits at an offering table. She wears a long wig with a tress falling over the front of the collar, and a long, tight dress with shoulder straps. Her left hand is placed on her chest holding a folded cloth (?), while the right is extended towards an offering table laden with ten loaves of bread. Underneath the table, to the right is still visible the front part of a ewer, and to the left is the top part of a jar.

Two horizontal lines of relatively large hieroglyphs run the width of the stela at its top. They read: (1) *ḥtp dj nswt Jnpw tpj ḏw.f . . .* (2) *jm3ḫwt ḫr nṯr ᶜ3 Špsjt-k3w rn.s nfr Jr[jt]* '(1) An offering which the king gives and Anubis, who is on his hill (gives) . . . (2) the honoured one before the great god, Shepsit-kau, her beautiful name, Irit'. The offerings listed above the table are: *ḫ3 t ḫ3 ḥnqt ḫ3 šs ḫ3 3pd ḫ3 k3* 'A thousand of bread, a thousand of beer, a thousand of linen, a thousand of fowl and a thousand of oxen'. In front of the owner's face is written: *n jm3ḫwt Jrjt* 'to the honoured one, Irit'. To the right of the table is written *dpḥt ḥtp* 'food requirement'.

The identity of Shepsit-kau remains highly uncertain. Although her name was similar to that of Hesi-Min's wife (M22), no beautiful name was attested for the latter. At the same time, no titles are recorded on our stela for comparison. The style of relief of the stela suggests a later date than that of tomb M22, perhaps at the very end of the Old Kingdom, or immediately after. This dating is only tentative, for as similar pieces are published a relative dating may be possible.

THE COFFIN OF HETEPET

CG 28008[1]

Pls. 11, 12; Figs. 29, 30.

Ownership and Dating

In the absence of a complete publication of all the tombs at El-Hawawish and the coffins reported to have come from Akhmim, any comparative studies aiming at establishing the date of a coffin or the identity of its owner can only be tentative.

The name of Hetepet reminds one of that of Kheni's wife/daughter (H24).[2] The possibility of her identification with one of them merits consideration although it should be borne in mind that the name may well have been popular in this area at a certain time.

Like the wife of Kheni,[3] the owner of this coffin was a priestess of Hathor, and was described as both *ḫkrt nswt* 'royal ornament' and *ḫkrt nswt wꜥtt* 'sole royal ornament'. As for palaeographical details, one notices that the *n* is written with two parallel horizontal lines in its middle as is the case in the tomb and on the coffin of Tjeti (M8), father (?) of Kheni.[4] The *f*, on the other hand, is shown on our coffin with the head missing, which may indicate a later development from the head cut but drawn, as on Tjeti's coffin.[5] The sign for *tp* in *Jnpw tpj ḏw.f* (side 3 of coffin) is depicted with the beard across the cheeks and under the chin, which is a rather peculiar characteristic of the figure of Kheni himself.[6]

It is interesting to notice the palaeographical similarities between the inscriptions on this coffin and another (CG 28015),[7] found also at Akhmim and belonging to Henit; the latter is perhaps to be identified with Heni the wife/daughter of Kheni.[8] On both coffins, as on the false doors of the two women in Kheni's tomb,[9] the name Anubis is written without the jackal figure. On both coffins also (but not in the tomb) the *wt* in the epithet of Anubis *jmj wt* is written with the determinative , and the name of Hathor as .

If this identification is correct, then the coffin should be dated to the end of Dynasty 6.

Measurements

Length: 1.88m.
Width: .53m.
Height: .58m.

Workmanship

The four sides as well as the bottom of the coffin are formed of longitudinal planks of wood, in some cases irregular, joined together with internal wooden pegs and leather bindings. The bottom is fixed to the sides at right angles, with wooden pegs traversing sides 3 and 4 into the bottom planks. To strengthen the bottom two side strips of wood are added, and are attached to its planks with perpendicular pegs and to sides 3 and 4 with oblique ones.[10]

Decoration

The coffin is decorated on its four sides. The following figure shows the numbering of the sides and the direction of the inscriptions.

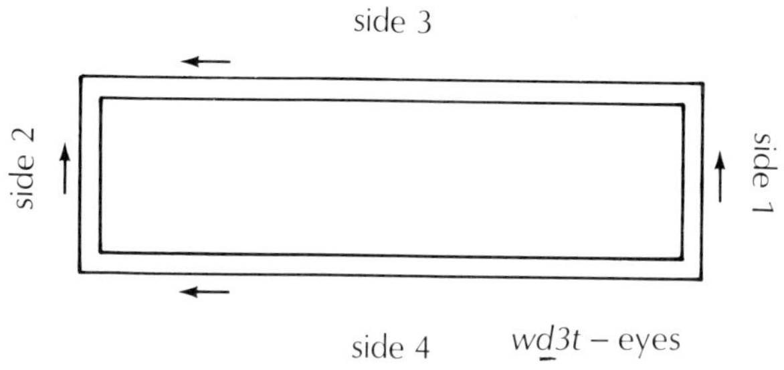

Side 1: There is one horizontal line of hieroglyphs which reads: *prt-ḫrw n jm3ḫwt ḫkrt nswt Ḥtp* 'may an invocation offering come forth for the honoured one, the royal ornament, Hetep'.

Side 2: One line of hieroglyphs is inscribed. It reads: *jm3ḫwt ḫr Jnpw ḥm(t)-nṯr Ḥwt-ḥr Ḥtp* 'the honoured one before Anubis, the priestess of Hathor, Hetep'.

Side 3: One horizontal line of text runs the length of the coffin, at its upper part: *ḥtp dj nswt Jnpw tpj ḏw.f jmj wt nb t3 ḏsr qrs.t(j).s nfr m jz.s n ḫrt-nṯr m zmjt jmntt ḫkrt nswt wʿtt Ḥtpt* 'An offering which the king gives and Anubis, who is on his hill, who is in the embalming place, lord of the sacred land (gives): that she be buried well in her tomb of the necropolis in the western desert. The sole royal ornament, Hetepet'.

Side 4: One horizontal line of hieroglyphs runs the length of the coffin, and reads: *ḥtp dj nswt Wsjr nb Ḏdw Ḫntj-jmntjw nb 3bḏw prt-ḫrw n.s m W3g m Ḏḥwtjt ḥm(t)-nṯr Ḥwt-ḥr nbt nht Ḥtpt* 'An offering which the king gives and Osiris, lord of Busiris, and Khentiamentiu, lord of Abydos (give). May an invocation offering come forth for her at the Wag-feast, and at the Thot-feast. The priestess of Hathor lady of the sycamore, Hetepet'.

Below this line, the *wḏ3t*-eyes are painted at the right. The rest of this side is occupied by an offering list arranged in two registers of 34 entries each. Each item is preceded by two numbers: the first indicates its place in the register, beginning from right, the second, inserted between parentheses, refers to the number given by Barta to the same item.[11]

Register I

1 (1) *mw z3t* water for pouring
2 (2) *snṯr ḫt sḏt*[12] lighted incense
3 (3) *stj ḥb* oil
4 (4) *ḥknw* oil
5 (5) *sfṯ* oil
6 (6) *nḫnm* oil
7 (7) *tw3wt* oil
8 (8) *ḥ3tt nt ʿš* best cedar oil
9 (9) *(ḥ3tt)*[13] *nt ṯḥnw* best Libyan oil
10 (10) *ʿrf n w3ḏw* a bag of green paint
11 (11) *(ʿrf)*[14] *n msdmt* a bag of black paint
12 (12) *wnḫw* clothes material
13 (13) *snṯr ḫt sḏt* lighted incense
14 (14) *qbḥw (nṯrj) ṯ3 2* libation water and 2 balls (?) of natron
15 (15) *ḫ3wt rdjt prt-ḫrw* offering table, the giving of offerings
16 (16) *ḥtp nswt* royal offerings
17 (17) *ḥtp jmj wsḫt* offerings which are in the palace
18 (18) *ḥmsj jgr* a kind of food[15]
19 (19) *jʿw-r šns ḏwjw* breakfast bread and jug
20 (20) *t-(w)t wt*-bread
21 (21) *t-rtḥ rtḥ*-bread
22 (22) *nmst nt ḏsrt nmst*-jug of *ḏsrt*-beverage
23 (23) *(nmst)*[16]*nt ḫnqt-ḫnms*[17] *nmst*-jug of *ḫnms*-beer
24 (24) *šns* bread
25 (24) *ʿ n f3jt* serving bowl
26 (25) *šbw šns* main meal bread
27 (25) *šbw*[18] *ḏwjw* main meal jug
28 (26) *swt* piece of meat
29 (27) *mw ʿ.wj*[19] water, two bowls
30 (28) *bd ʿ.wj* natron, two bowls
31 (29) *jʿw-r šns* breakfast bread
32 (30) *t-(w)t wt*-bread
33 (31) *t-rtḥ rtḥ*-bread
34 (32) *ḥṯ3* bread

Register II

1 (33) *nḥrw* bread
2 (34) *dptj* bread
3 (35) *pzn* bread
4 (36) *šns* bread
5 (37) *t-jmj-t3* bread
6 (38) *ḫnfwt* bread
7 (39) *ḥbnnwt* bread
8 (40) *qmḥw* bread
9 (41) *jd3t ḥ3.k ḥm-k3* bread, (place it) behind you, ka-servant
10 (42) *p3wt* bread
11 (43) *t-3šr* bread
12 (44) *ḥḏw* onions

13 (45) *ḫpš* foreleg
14 (46) *jwˁ* piece of meat
15 (47) *zḫn* piece of meat
16 (48) *sw̌t* piece of meat
17 (49) *spḥt* piece of the ribs
18 (50) *3šrt* roasted piece of meat
19 (51, 52) *mjzt nnšm* liver, spleen
20 (53, 54) *ḥˁ jwf* piece of meat
21 (54) *n ḥ3t*(20) brisket
22 (55) *r* goose
23 (56) *ṯrp* goose
24 (58) *sr* goose
25 (57) *mz3t* goose
26 (59) *mnwt* pigeon
27 (60) *t-zjf* pastry
28 (61) *šˁwt* pastry
29 (62) *np3wt ˁ.wj* pastry, two bowls
30 (63) *mswt ˁ.wj* pastry, two bowls
31 (64) *ḏsrt ˁ.wj* beverage, two bowls
32 (65) *j3tt ˁ.wj* beverage, two bowls
33 (66) *ḥnqt-ḫnms ḫnms*-beer
34 *n ẖkrt nsw̌t Ḥtpt* for the royal ornament, Hetepet.

NOTES

1. A description of this coffin and a transcription of its text have been published in Lacau, *Sarcophages* 1, 22-24.
2. *El-Hawawish* 2, 9. See also the coffin of *Ḥtpjt* (the Liverpool Museum – 13.10.11.26. The information on this coffin was kindly supplied by the authorities of the Museum). However, the title *wršt Mnw* recorded on the coffin is absent from the inscriptions of tomb H24.
3. Ibid 2, fig. 23.
4. Ibid 3, figs. 13, 15-17.
5. Ibid 3, figs. 15, 16.
6. Ibid 2, figs. 8, 11, 15, 21.
7. Lacau, *Sarcophages* 1, 34.
8. *El-Hawawish* 2, 10.
9. Ibid 2, figs. 4, 23.
10. For details and diagrams see Lacau, *Sarcophages* 1, 23, 24, et passim.
11. Barta, *Opferliste,* 47-50, 84-86.
12. Barta, ibid, 84, n. 149, noticed that *ḫt* and *sḏt* are sometimes used in the same list for items 2 and 13, as e.g. in Davies, *Sheikh Saïd,* pl. 26, where *ḫt* is used for no. 2 and *sḏt* in no. 13. In our list, however, *ḫt* and *sḏt* are both written for each of items 2 and 13.
13. *ḫ3tt* is written only once for both items 8 and 9. But, unlike the more usual writing of these items (Barta, *Opferliste,* 182, fig. 5; *El-Hawawish* 3, fig. 17), *nt* is repeated in each case.
14. *ˁrf* is written only once above items 10 and 11.
15. Barta renders as 'sitz nieder und schweige' *(Opferliste,* 85). For comments see *El-Hawawish* 1, 37, n. 99.
16. *nmst* is given once for items 22 and 23.
17. For the reading of *ḫnms,* compare with Register II, item 33.
18. *šbw* extends over items 26 and 27.
19. The reading of *mwˁˁ* is also possible.
20. *jwf n ḥ3t* begins in compartment no. 20 and continues in no. 21.

THE COFFIN OF SHEPSI-PU-MIN

CG 28016[1]

Pls. 13, 14; Figs. 31, 32.

Ownership and Dating

The two names of the owner of this coffin, Shepsi and Shepsi-pu-Min, may suggest a possible relationship with, or at least a closeness in date to the nomarchic family at Akhmim at the end of the Old Kingdom. Shepsi was the name of a son of the owner of tomb M8,[2] and Shepsi-pu-Min was the name of the owner of tomb H24,[3] as well as that of the owner of another coffin from Akhmim,[4] who might have been one and the same as the nomarch Bekhen.[5] Like members of this family, our Shepsi-pu-Min also held the titles of *ḥ3tj-ᶜ smr wᶜtj* and *sḏ3wtj-bjtj* 'count, sole companion' and 'treasurer of the king of Lower Egypt'. Yet as none of the above-mentioned individuals appears to have carried the two names written on the coffin, it seems unlikely that the owner of our coffin is to be directly identified with any of them.

The reference on the coffin to Osiris as both lord of Busiris and lord of Abydos may be of some significance for the purpose of dating. Only two other coffins known to have come from Akhmim,[6] and one tomb so far found at El-Hawawish, are inscribed with this reference to Osiris. The tomb belongs to Nebet, whom I dated to the first half of Pepy II's reign.[7] However, the palaeographical details on the coffin under consideration may suggest a later date, perhaps Dynasty 8 – First Intermediate Period. An analysis of these details is reserved until all coffins from the site have been copied and studied.

Measurements

Length: 1.84m.
Width: .57m.
Height: .56m. (without bottom), plus lid .035m.

Workmanship

The sides are formed each of three or four irregular planks of wood, the lid is formed of two planks and the bottom is now missing. The planks are linked together by means of internal wooden pegs, and gaps are filled with plaster. Two side strips are fixed to the inner side of the lid, one at each end. They are of the same width as the inside of the coffin and thus prevent the sliding of the lid. Each strip is attached to the lid planks with three leather bindings. The bottom must have had three similar side strips, judging by the holes for the oblique pegs in sides 3 and 4.[8]

Decoration

The coffin is decorated on its four sides as well as on the external surface of the lid. The following figure shows the direction of the writing. Each side, except side 4, has one horizontal line of text.

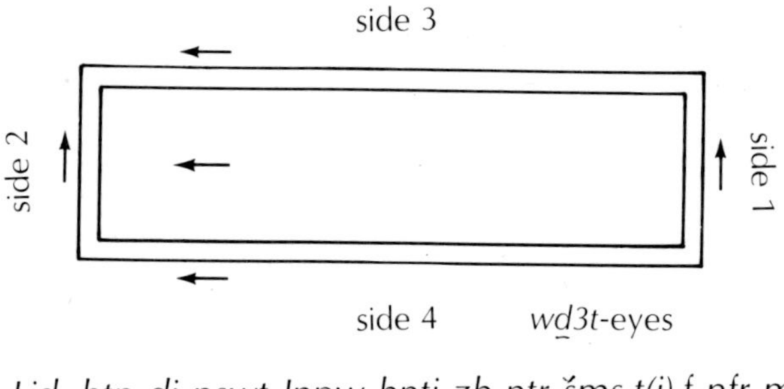

Lid: ḥtp dj nswt Jnpw ḫntj zḥ-nṯr šms.t(j).f nfr m zmjt m [jmn]tt jm3ḫw Špsj 'An offering which the king gives and Anubis foremost of the divine booth (gives): that he be accompanied well in the desert in the west, the honoured one, Shepsi'.

Side 1: jm3ḫw ḫr nṯr ˁ3 sḏ3wtj-bjtj Špsj 'the honoured one before the great god, the treasurer of the king of Lower Egypt, Shepsi'.

Side 2: prt-ḫrw n ḥ3tj-ˁ sḏ3wtj-bjtj Špsj-pw-Mnw 'may an invocation offering come forth for the count, the treasurer of the king of Lower Egypt, Shepsi-pu-Min'.

Side 3: ḥtp dj nswt Jnpw tpj ḏw.f jmj wt nb t3 ḏsr qrst nfrt m jz.f n ḫrt-nṯr ḥ3tj-ˁ smr wˁtj ḫrj-ḥbt 'An offering which the king gives and Anubis, who is on his hill, who is in the embalming place, lord of the sacred land (gives), of a good burial in his tomb of the necropolis. The count, the sole companion, the lector priest'.

Side 4: This side has, like the others, one horizontal line of hieroglyphs in its upper part. Below this, at the right, the *wḏ3t*-eyes are painted, but with no offering list. The text reads: *ḥtp dj nswt Wsjr nb Ḏdw nb 3bḏw*(9) *prt-ḫrw n.f m W3g Ḏḥwtjt n ḥ3tj-ˁ sḏ3wtj-bjtj Špsj-pw-Mnw* 'An offering which the king gives and Osiris, lord of Busiris and lord of Abydos (gives). May an invocation offering come forth for him at the Wag-feast and the Thot-feast, (for)(10) the count, the treasurer of the king of Lower Egypt, Shepsi-pu-Min'.

NOTES

1. For a previous description of this coffin and a copy of its inscriptions, mostly in standard hieroglyphs, see Lacau, *Sarcophages* 1, 35, 36.
2. *El-Hawawish* 3, fig. 13.
3. Ibid 2, passim.
4. Lacau, *Sarcophages* 1, 29 – CG 28012.
5. This identification was made by Newberry, *LAAA* 4 [1912], 100. For the tomb of Bekhen see now *El-Hawawish* 1, 38ff.
6. These belong to *Snt/Mrwt* (Lacau, *Sarcophages* 1, 28 – CG 28011) and *Ḥtpjt* (the Liverpool Museum – 13.10.11.26. I am grateful to authorities of the Liverpool Museum for information regarding this coffin). This is the same as coffin no. 2 of Newberry, *LAAA* 4 [1912], 120, but the reference to it being in the Cairo Museum should be corrected as it is in the Liverpool Museum.
7. *El-Hawawish* 3, 38, fig. 27.
8. Lacau, *Sarcophages* 1, 35, 36.
9. See n. 6 above.
10. This *n* is superfluous since the *prt-ḫrw* is said to be *n.f.*

TOMBS M27, M28 and M29

Ownership and Date

The three tombs are now completely uninscribed. Their location, in the forecourt of M22, may suggest, however, that they belonged to relatives, or to contemporaries of Hesi-Min. This may also be gleaned from the style of their false doors – consistently the simple type used by Hesi-Min – and the pottery sherds – similar to those found in M22.

Suggested date: Probably end of Dynasty 5 or shortly after.

TOMB M27

Figs. 1 – 5.

I ARCHITECTURAL FEATURES

M27 is the northernmost of three small tombs cut into the east wall of the forecourt of M22. Only the lower portion of the façade and walls of this tomb remain, the upper part and the ceiling being completely gone so no measurement of the original height is possible. The walls survive only to a height of 1.00m. to approximately 1.60m., and it is possible that the ceiling was not much higher than 1.60m. Above this height the west wall now opens into the forecourt of M22, while the north wall issues into the chapel of M22 and the east wall into the chapel of M21. Although the upper part of the south wall is also missing, there is no damage in the lower section which forms also the north wall of adjacent tomb M28.

In the façade of M27 to the north of its entrance is a small, uninscribed false door above Pit e in the forecourt of M22. The doorway measures .60m. wide x .45m. thick. Judging from the entrances of the two small tombs to its south, M28 and M29, it can be conjectured that the doorway of M27 originally may have been surmounted by a drum and lintel. The entrance gives access to a nearly square tomb measuring 2.60m. N-S, by 2.60m. on the north wall and 2.70m. on the south wall. All four walls were well cut with clean, vertical lines and smooth surfaces, but show no sign of having been plastered or painted. Into the floor are cut two shafts and above each in the north wall is a small, uninscribed false door. That at the western end of the north wall is .94m. high x .46m. wide; that at the eastern end is 1.27m. high x .62m. wide.

II BURIAL APARTMENTS

Two shafts, both found plundered, are cut into the floor of M27.

I A vertical shaft cut into the NW corner has a mouth .90m. square and a depth of 2.55m. At the floor of the shaft an entrance .70m. wide x .75m. high opens into the north wall. A step down, .10m. in height, leads to a rectangular-shaped burial chamber 2.00m. N-S x .90m. E-W at the north wall x 1.00m. high at the north wall. The ceiling, as well as the east and north walls are well cut and straight, but the floor is uneven with a slight downward slope in its southern half.

II In the NE corner is cut a vertical shaft with a mouth 1.00m. square and a depth of 2.80m. In the north wall at the floor of the shaft an entry .70m. wide x .90m. high leads to a rectangular burial chamber 2.30m. N-S x .90m. E-W x .90m. high. It is very well cut, but has soft corners where the ceiling meets the north wall.

TOMB M28

Figs. 1 – 3.

I ARCHITECTURAL FEATURES

Tomb M28 is also cut into the east wall of the forecourt of M22, lying adjacent to and directly south of M27. Its doorway measures .60m. wide x .95m. thick x 1.15m. high. It is surmounted by a small drum .15m. high and, above that, an undecorated lintel .35m. high. The floor of the entrance slopes upward and inward at a 5° angle. The tomb is basically rectangular in shape, measuring 2.65m. N-S on the east wall, 2.60m. N-S on the west wall, 1.80m. E-W on the south wall, and 1.70m. E-W on the north wall. The entire southern half is rough and incomplete, with sections of rock at floor level left uncut. The tomb shows no sign of having been plastered or painted. One shaft lies almost in the centre of the tomb.

II BURIAL APARTMENT

I This is a vertical shaft with a mouth .95m. square and a depth of 1.50m. from the highest floor level. At the floor of the shaft an entrance .75m. high is cut the width of the north wall, leading to a small burial chamber .80m. N-S x 1.35m. E-W x .75m. high. The north wall slopes slightly inward at the ceiling.

TOMB M29

Figs. 1 – 3, 5.

I ARCHITECTURAL FEATURES

Adjacent to tomb M28, this is the southernmost of the three tombs cut into the east wall of the forecourt of M22. The doorway measures .60m. wide x .85m. thick x 1.30m. high. It is surmounted by a drum .30m. high (shaped only from the outside), above which are two almost identical lintels, the lower one projecting from the façade slightly more than the upper one. Each lintel measures 1.00m. wide x .30m. high. The tomb itself is rectangular in shape, measuring 3.70m. E-W x 2.00m. N-S x 1.35m. high. In the east end of the north wall is cut a recess, 1.50m. E-W x 1.20m. N-S, into which is cut Shaft III. Two other shafts are contiguous with the south wall, and above each of the three shafts is a small uninscribed false door. That above Shaft I measures .95m. high x .69m. wide, the one above Shaft II is 1.08m. high x .70m. wide, while that above Shaft III is .96m. high x .68m. wide. The tomb is all of rough texture and shows no sign of having been plastered or painted. The floor is uneven and a small portion of rock in the SE corner has been left uncut.

II BURIAL APARTMENTS

Three shafts are cut into the floor of this tomb, all being found plundered.

I Shaft I is located to the south of the entrance in front of the west wall and contiguous to the south wall. This deep vertical shaft has a mouth 1.00m. square and a depth of 6.00m. At the floor of the shaft in the east wall is cut a small niche .90m. high x .75m. wide x .20m. deep with the back wall sloping outward towards the top. In the floor of the shaft a small step down of .10m. leads to the floor of a rectangular-shaped burial chamber cut into the west wall. It measures 1.30m. E-W x 1.35m. N-S x 1.00m. high. The ceiling is level, but the floor is horizontal for a length of 1.00m., then slants upwards to a recess in the west wall which is .30m. deep. The south wall is incomplete, being well cut for .25m. below the ceiling, but the remaining uncut portion projects, resulting in an uneven wall. The shaft, niche and burial chamber are all well cut. A wooden face and hand belonging to a coffin were found in the filling of the shaft, indicating an intrusive burial of later date, probably Roman, which was also plundered.

II Not very well-preserved, this shaft lies in the eastern end of the tomb, contiguous with the south wall. It is a vertical shaft with a mouth 1.00m. square and a depth of 4.00m. A burial chamber cut into the south wall has an almost rectangular shape, but its floor, ceiling and walls have clean angles. It measures .80m. N-S x 1.80m. E-W x 1.05m. high. Part of the shaft floor is included in the area of the burial chamber.

III A vertical shaft is located in the recess cut into the north wall of the tomb. Its mouth is 1.00m. square and its depth is 2.35m. An opening in the north wall .80m. high leads to a nearly rectangular burial chamber which is very well cut. It measures .85m. N-S x 1.20m. E-W x .80m. high.

III FINDS

Wooden Objects

Pl. 9d.

H82 M29 01: A wooden male face, 23.5cm. long, with painted details was found in the debris which filled Shaft I of tomb M29. It belonged most probably to an anthropoid coffin of a much later (Roman?) intrusive burial, which was itself plundered in turn. The face was presumably fixed to the flat lid of the coffin with three vertical wooden pegs.

H82 M29 02: A wooden hand, 17.5cm. long, with painted details was found with the above-mentioned face, and probably belonged to the same coffin. It was fixed to the lid with one wooden peg (unless there was another peg in the missing part of the hand).

TOMB H14

I ARCHITECTURAL FEATURES

Fig. 33.

Tomb H14 is located in the southwest face of the mountain at a height of 230 metres above mean sea level. Incomplete in both its forecourt and chapel areas, it lies directly north of, and is probably not far removed in time from, the tomb of Kheni-Ankhu (H15), which was also unfinished.

The Forecourt and Portico

The face of the mountain has been cut down to a depth of approximately 2.00m. to form a forecourt area and a portico. The forecourt area is incomplete with the southern end largely uncut, and access to it is rough and very steep. Some areas of the uncut rock have the appearance of steps, which perhaps were only to facilitate the original excavation of this tomb. The forecourt area is defined by two side walls and measures 5.20m. E-W x an average of 1.40m. N-S. The floor, with a rough unfinished surface, slopes downward at a 5° angle to the portico. Two sloping passages are cut into the forecourt area, one in the middle of the west wall, and the other at the southern end of the east wall. Each of these has a recessed entry defined by a doorway.

Cut in the mother rock, the portico measures 5.10m. E-W x 1.80m. N-S. It has two engaged pillars, .65m. N-S x .20m. E-W, and two free-standing pillars, .65m. square, all of which are 2.00m. in height. The well preserved pillars have sharp edges and lines, and they support a lintel .35m. high which extends the full width of the portico. On a line with the north side of the pillars a small step, .10m. in height, leads down to the floor of the portico area, which has a downward slope of 5° towards the entrance. The height of the portico at the entrance wall is 2.20m. The entire portico area is sharply and cleanly cut on all its surfaces. In the east wall is cut a niche .60m. wide x .20m. deep.

The Chapel

The main entrance to the tomb is cut into the centre of the north wall of the portico, opposite the two free-standing pillars. The entry is defined by an external door recess 1.65m. wide x .15m. deep. From this recess a small step, .10m. high, leads down to the level floor of the doorway which measures .80m. wide x .75m. thick x 1.75m. high below a very large drum .50m. high. A small step up, .10m. high, gives direct access to Sloping Passage II in a very small and incomplete chamber. Rough cuttings in small areas to the east and west of the sloping passage would indicate some excavation was begun, but abandoned. Also, to the left of the doorway are a few well executed corners cut to a ceiling height of 1.60m. This chamber is so rough and shapeless that it cannot be measured. In no part of this tomb is there evidence of any decoration.

The Side Chamber

Into the west wall of the portico is cut an entrance leading to a secondary chamber. The doorway measures .65m. wide x .50m. thick x 1.10m. high, and is surmounted by a lintel .35m. in height. The floor of the entrance slopes slightly downward for .50m. to a chamber basically rectangular in shape, the east wall being at a 120° angle to the north wall. The chamber measures 2.80m. on the south wall, 1.90m. on the west wall, 2.25m. on the north wall and 1.35m. on the east wall, and 1.90m. high. Into the centre of the northern half of the room is cut Sloping Passage I.

II BURIAL APARTMENTS

Two sloping passages are cut into the forecourt, and two more into the tomb itself. All were found plundered, but it appears that Sloping Passage I was re-used in a later period.

Inside the Tomb

I In the side chamber at the western end of the portico, Sloping Passage I is cut into the centre of the floor and into the north wall. It is oriented N-S with a mouth measuring 1.50m. x .75m, its northern end lying in a recess in the north wall, .60m. deep x .90m. high. It descends for 2.70m. at an angle of 45°, then changes to an angle of 20° for a further 1.00m. It terminates in a short horizontal passage .65m. long x .80m. wide x .80m. high. This opens into a rectangular burial chamber 2.20m. N-S x 1.70m. E-W x .85m. high. It is well cut and well preserved but the composition of the rock gives the surfaces an uneven texture. This burial chamber was disturbed. However, in it was found a large part of the wooden lid of a coffin, possibly from the Roman period, indicating that the burial chamber was re-used in a later period. There was no evidence of human remains.

II Just inside the main entrance of the tomb, and axial to it, is cut Sloping Passage II. It has a rectangular mouth measuring 1.40m. N-S x .80m. E-W. The passage descends for 2.70m. at a 35° angle, continuing at a 45° angle for a further length of 1.00m. At the floor of the passage is a rectangular burial chamber with a sloping ceiling, which is well cut and well preserved. It measures 2.35m. N-S x .65m. E-W x 1.30m. high at the entrance, and .90m. high at the north wall.

Outside the Tomb

(a) In the middle of the west wall of the forecourt is a sloping passage, its mouth being cut entirely within the west wall. Above its mouth and contiguous with its sides, the wall is cut back deeply to form a recess

1.05m. high. The entrance to this recess measures .65m. wide x 1.05m. high and is surmounted by a drum .25m. high, but has no lintel. The mouth of the sloping passage is basically rectangular in shape, although the west end is not cut parallel to the east end. It measures 1.20m. on the north side, .65m. on the east side, 1.05m. on the south side and .70m. on the west side. The passage descends directly from the doorway at a 55° angle for a length of 1.35m. to the floor of a burial chamber. The burial chamber, oriented E-W, is rectangular in shape with a small slope in the ceiling and is cleanly cut and well preserved. It measures 2.10m. E-W x 1.20m. N-S x .75m. high at the west wall.

(b) Sloping Passage (b) is cut partly into the floor and partly into the eastern wall of the forecourt at its SE corner. Its mouth measures 1.65m. E-W x .60m. on the west side and .70m. on the east side. As with Sloping Passage (a), the forecourt wall has been cut back above the mouth to form a deep recess. The entrance of the recess measures .65m. wide x 1.05m. high and is surmounted by a drum .35m. high. Below the drum a ceiling 1.05m. high curves to meet the back wall, forming a recess .90m. deep. Above the drum is a lintel .17m. high which projects from the façade by .05m. and which spans the full length of the east wall south of the engaged pillar. The passage descends for .90m. at a 35° angle, followed by a vertical drop of .35m. and a horizontal level of .30m., continuing at a 35° angle for another .90m. At the floor of the passage is a rectangular burial chamber, 2.10m. E-W x 1.15m. N-S x .90m. high.

III FINDS

Wooden Objects

Pl. 9e.

H82 H14 06: The upper half of the lid belonging to an anthropoid coffin of a much later intrusive burial, which was also disturbed, was found in the burial chamber of Sloping Passage I. All details were fixed to the lid with wooden pegs, three for the face and two for each of the hair locks and the hands. Traces of paint remain on the face and hands. Present measurements: .93m. long and .48m. wide.

Pottery

Fig. 34.

H82 H14 01: Bag-shaped jar. Most of rim missing. Nile silt, well fired. Simple wheel made, base cut flat, excess clay cut away. Red slip. H. 15.1cm. D. of rim undetermined. BW. 10.2cm. Th. varies from .6cm. at neck to 1.6cm. at base.

H82 H14 02: Globular jar. Badly broken. Nile silt, well fired. Simple wheel made, base cut and smoothed. Rope impressions at widest point. Red slip. Present height 18.8cm. D. of rim undetermined. BW. est. at 17.5cm. Th. varies from .5cm. at neck to 1.9cm. at base.

H82 H14 03: Bag-shaped jar. Rim chipped. Nile silt, evenly fired. Simple wheel made, round base cut and smoothed. H. 14.5cm. D. of rim 8.2cm. BW. 11.2cm. Th. varies from .5cm. at neck to 1.9cm. at base.

H82 H14 04: Conical jar. Most of rim missing. Nile silt, unevenly fired. Hand modelled in 2 sections. Thick black core. H. 25.1cm. D. of rim est. 11.2cm. BW. 12.5cm. Th. varies from .6cm. at neck to 2.1cm. at base.

H82 H14 05: Bag-shaped jar. Rim missing. Nile silt, evenly fired, very thin black core. Simple wheel made, round base cut and smoothed. Red slip. Present height 16.7cm. D. of rim undetermined. BW. 13.5cm. Th. varies from .6cm. at neck to 1.9cm. at base.

Pl. 1. Hesi-Min, chapel, south wall

Pl. 2. Hesi-Min, chapel, west wall

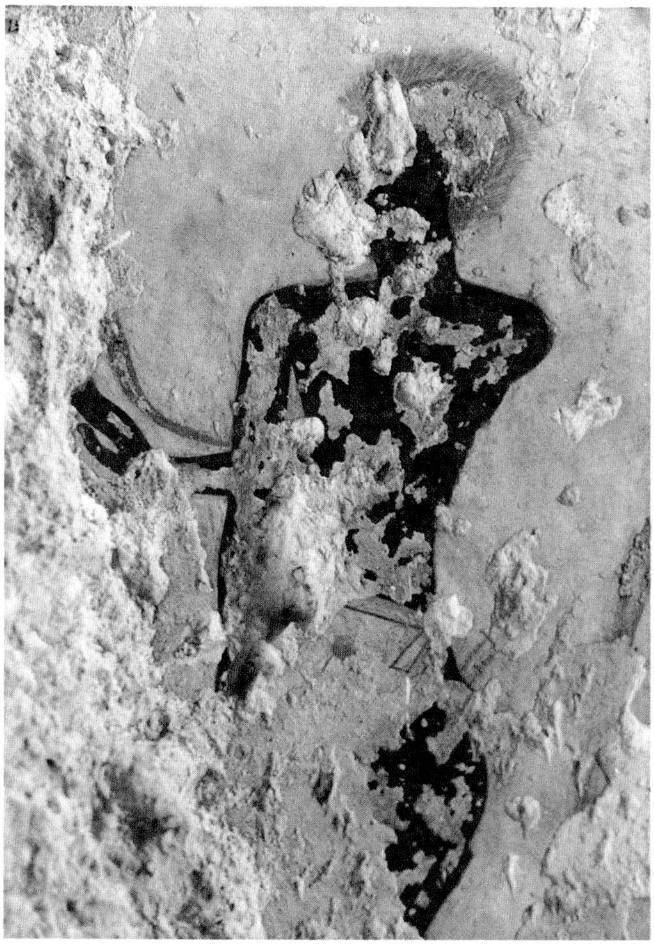

(a) south wall, register V

(b) south wall, register IV

(c) south wall, register II

(d) west wall, below the boat

Pl. 3. Hesi-Min, chapel, details

Pl. 4. Hesi-Min, shrine, false door

(a) right door thickness, top

(b) right door thickness, bottom

(c) left door thickness

Pl. 5. Hesi-Min, entrance

(b) east wall, statue niche

(a) north wall, remains of statue niche

Pl. 6. Hesi-Min, chapel

(a) north wall

(b) east wall, upper left

Pl. 7. Hesi-Min, shrine

(a) east wall, upper centre

(b) east wall, right

Pl. 8. Hesi-Min, shrine

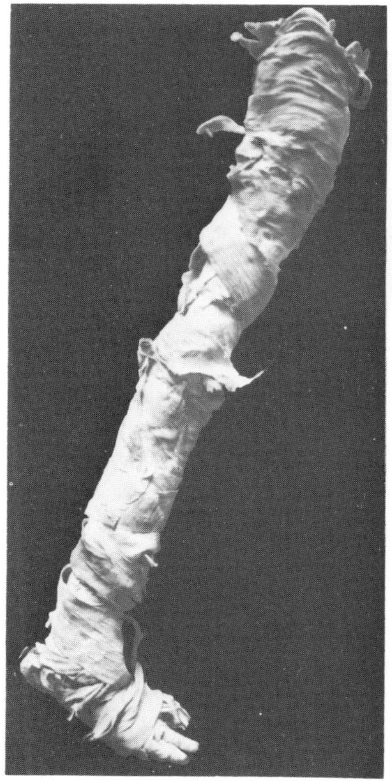
(a) Hesi-Min, leg

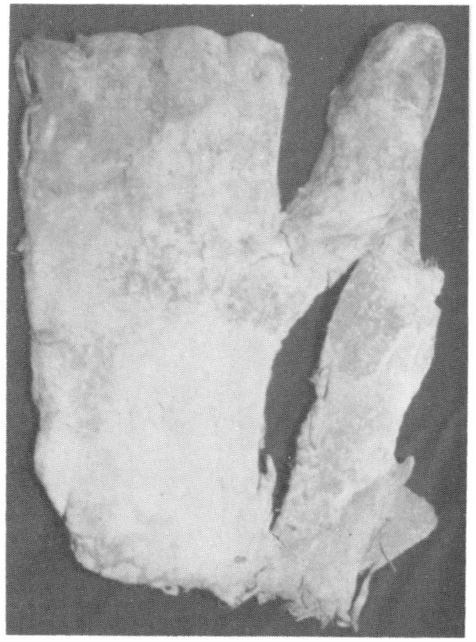
(b) Hesi-Min, bandages of the left hand

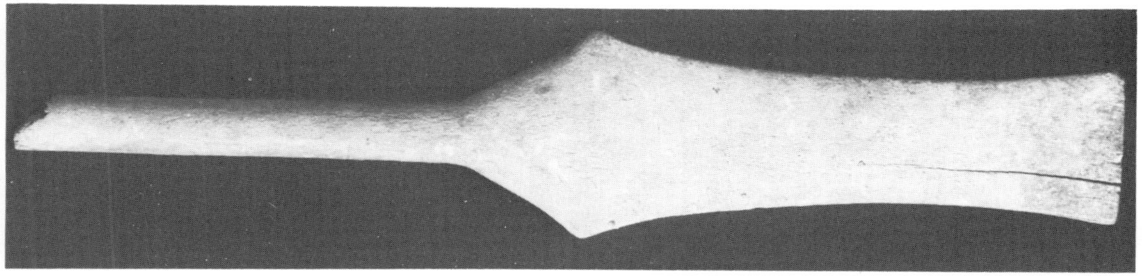
(c) Hesi-Min, sceptre

(d) wooden face and hand, H82 M29 01, H82 M29 02

(e) coffin lid, H82 H14 06

Pl. 9. Finds

Pl. 10. Shepsit-kau, stela

(a) side 1

(b) side 2

Pl. 11. Hetepet, coffin

Fig. 16. Hesi-Min, shrine, north wall

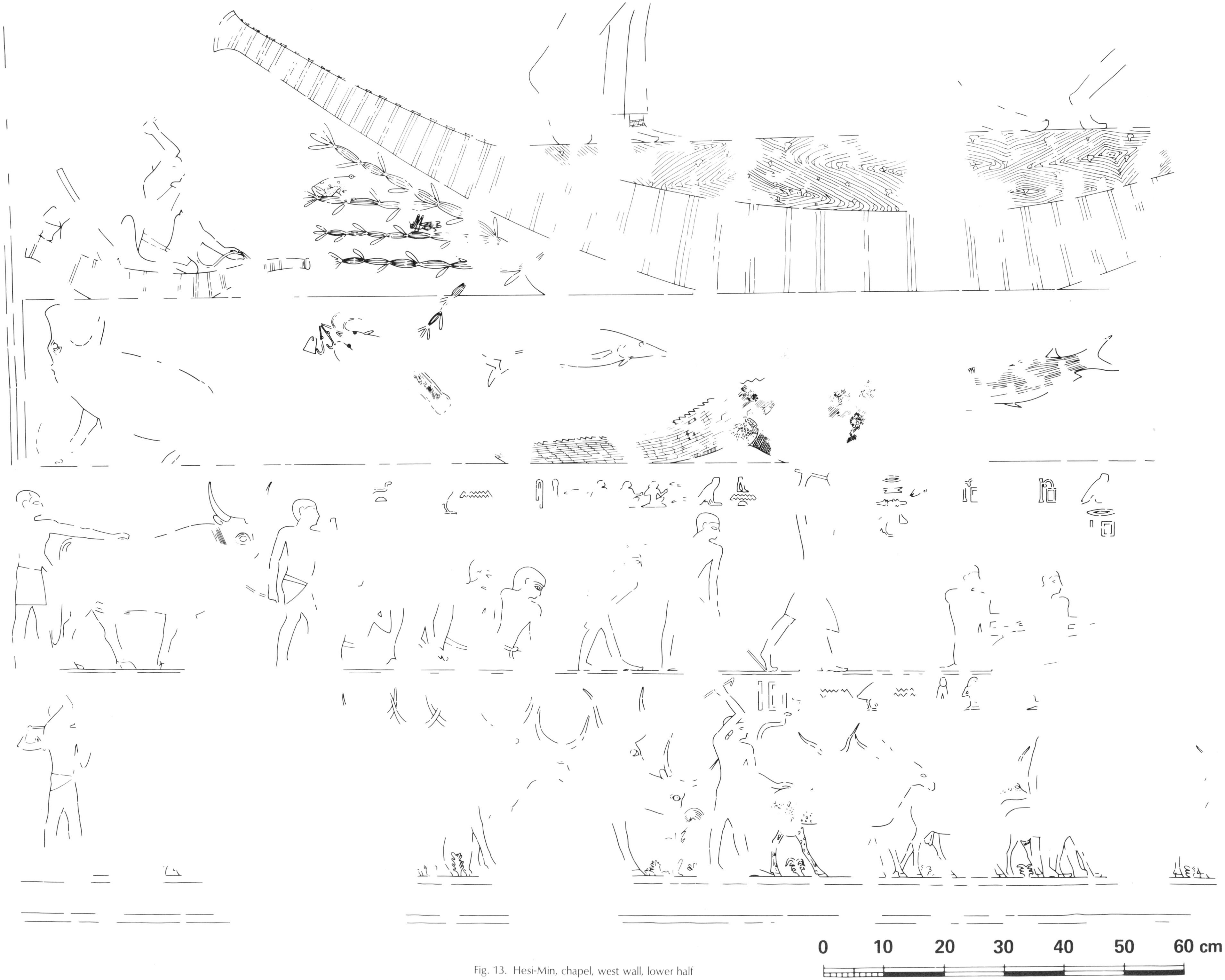

Fig. 13. Hesi-Min, chapel, west wall, lower half

Fig. 12. Hesi-Min, chapel, west wall

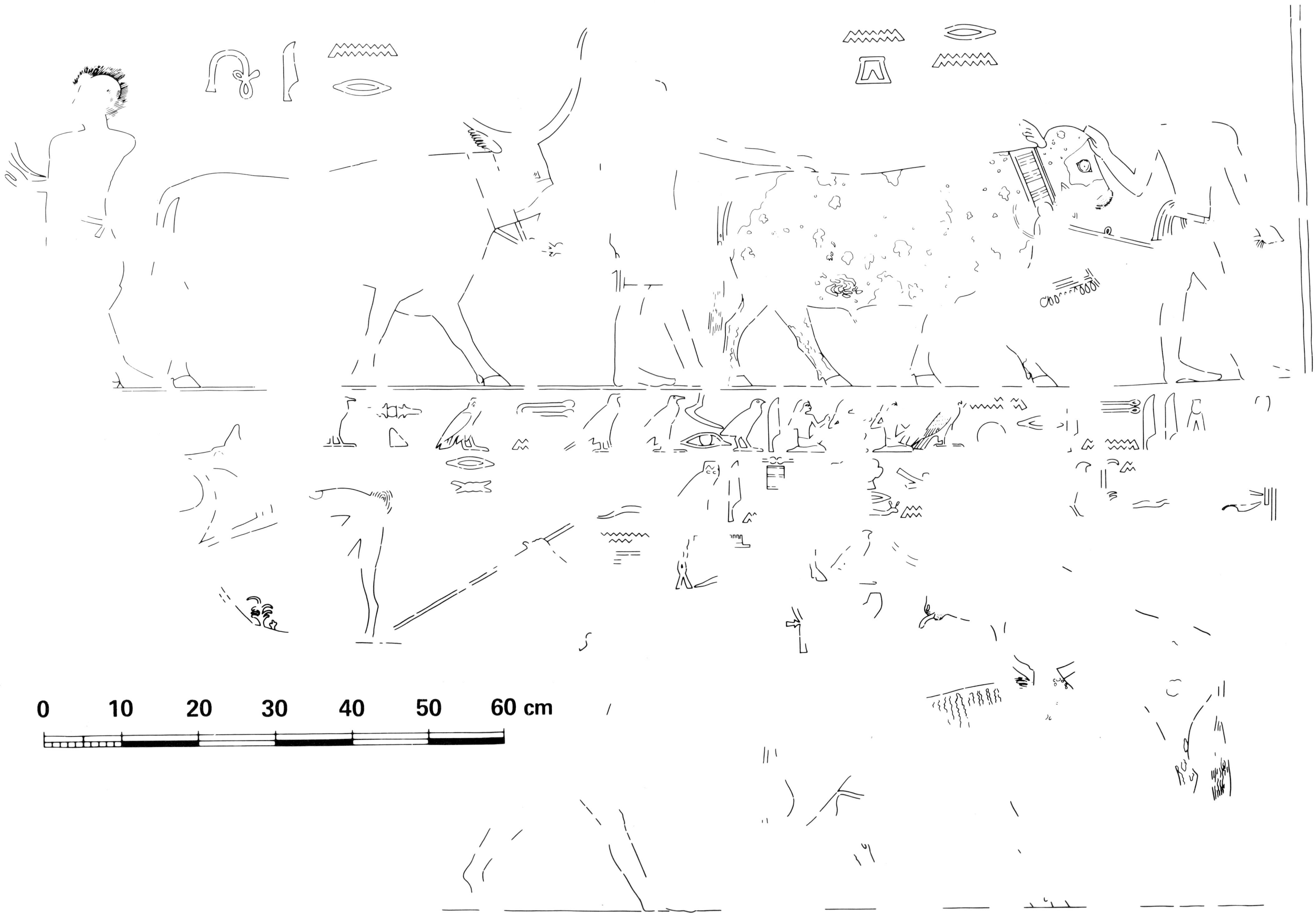

Fig. 11. Hesi-Min, chapel, south wall, west of entrance, lower right

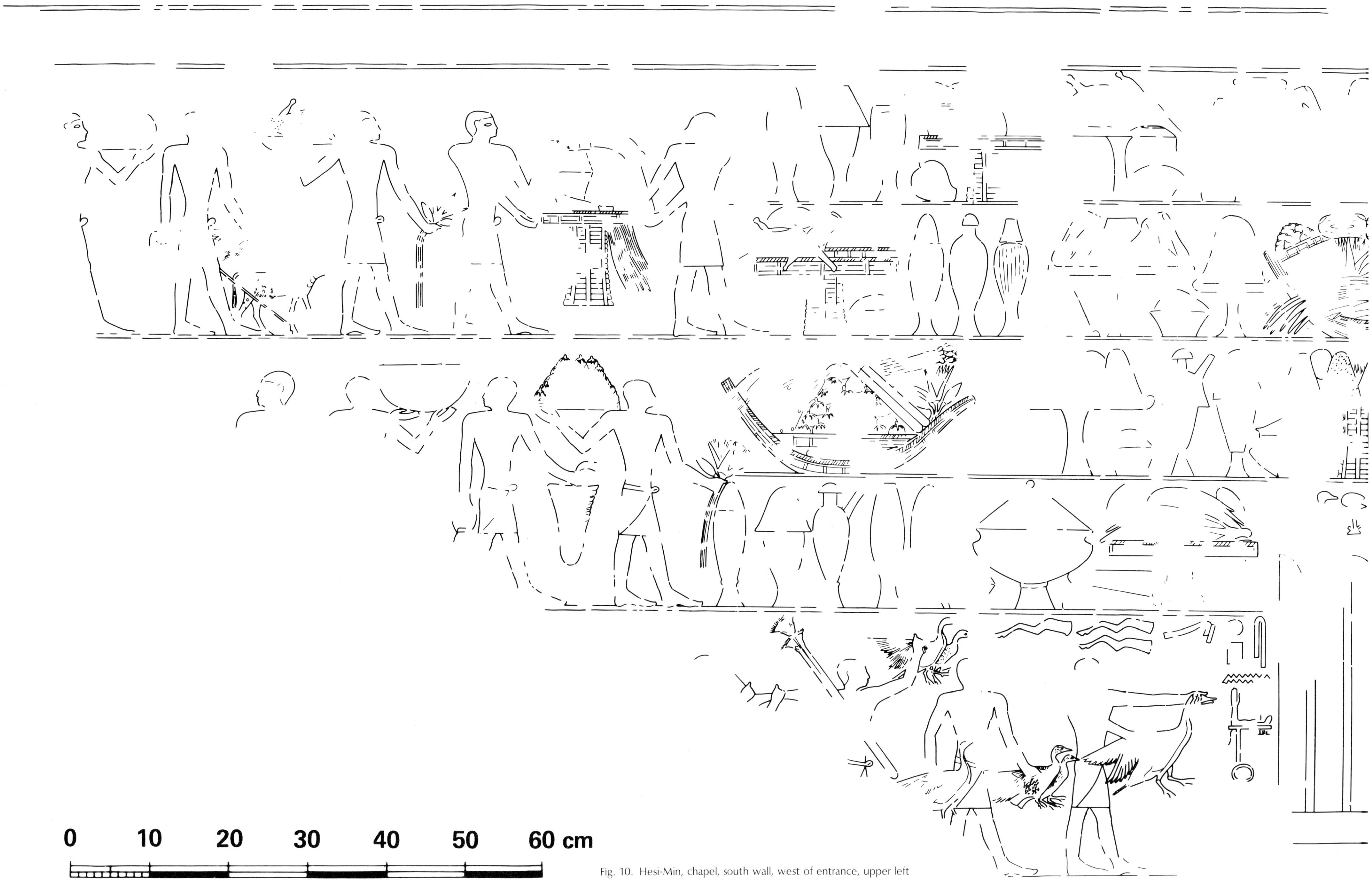

0 10 20 30 40 50 60 cm

Fig. 10. Hesi-Min, chapel, south wall, west of entrance, upper left

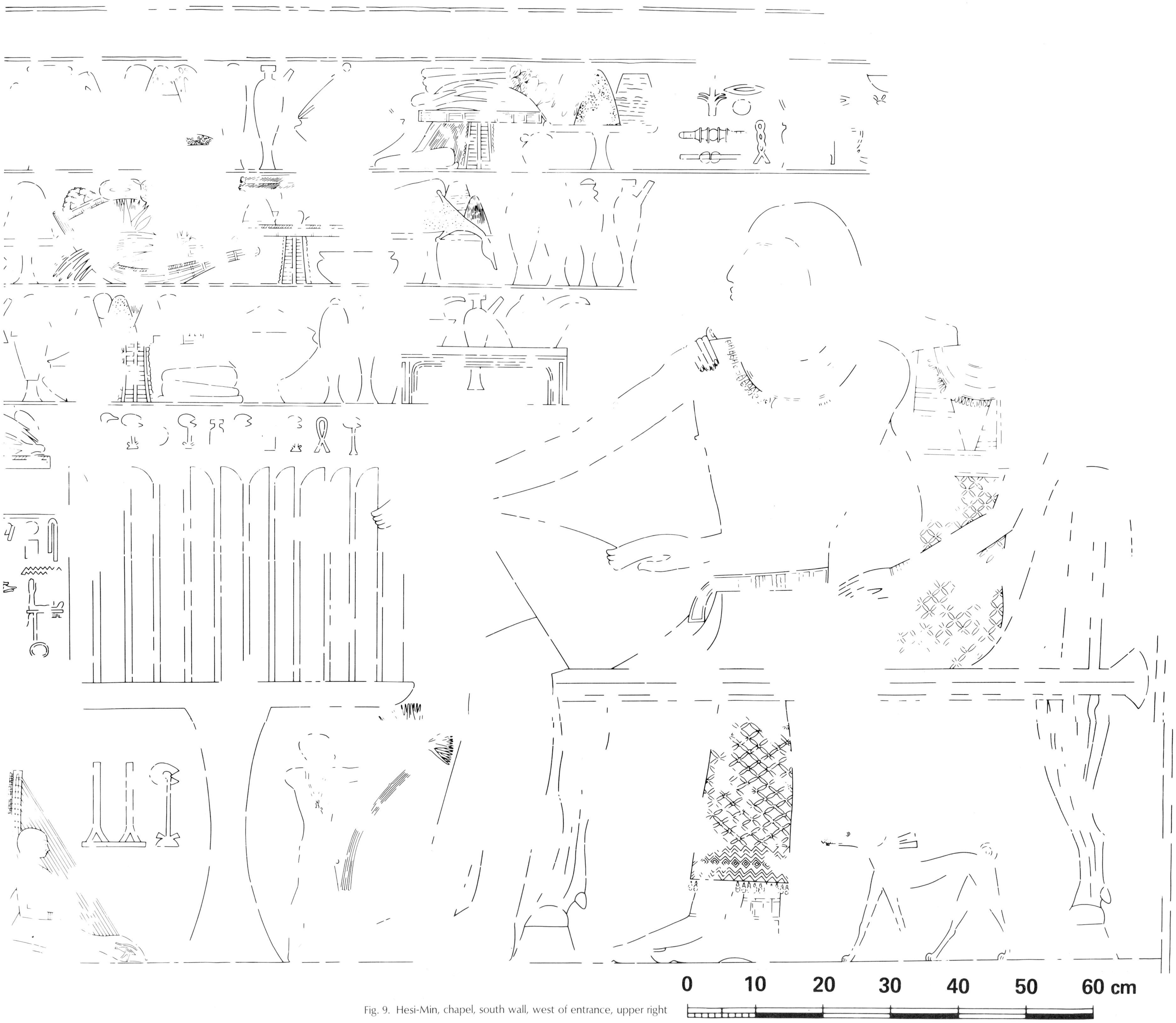

Fig. 9. Hesi-Min, chapel, south wall, west of entrance, upper right

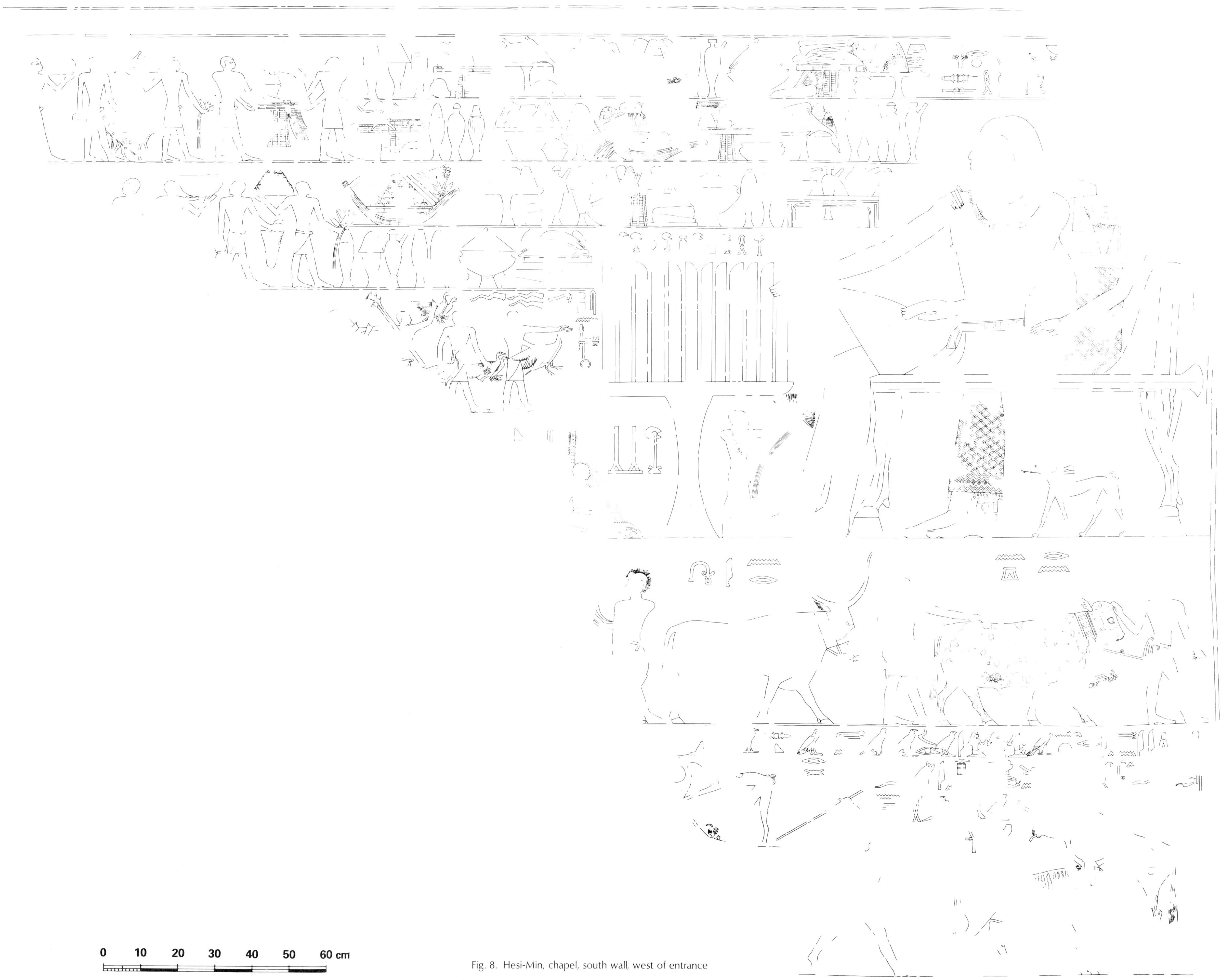

Fig. 8. Hesi-Min, chapel, south wall, west of entrance

(a) side 1

(b) side 2

Pl. 13. Shepsi-pu-Min, coffin

(a) lid

(b) side 3

(c) side 4

Pl. 14. Shepsi-pu-Min, coffin

Fig. 14. Hesi-Min, chapel, east wall

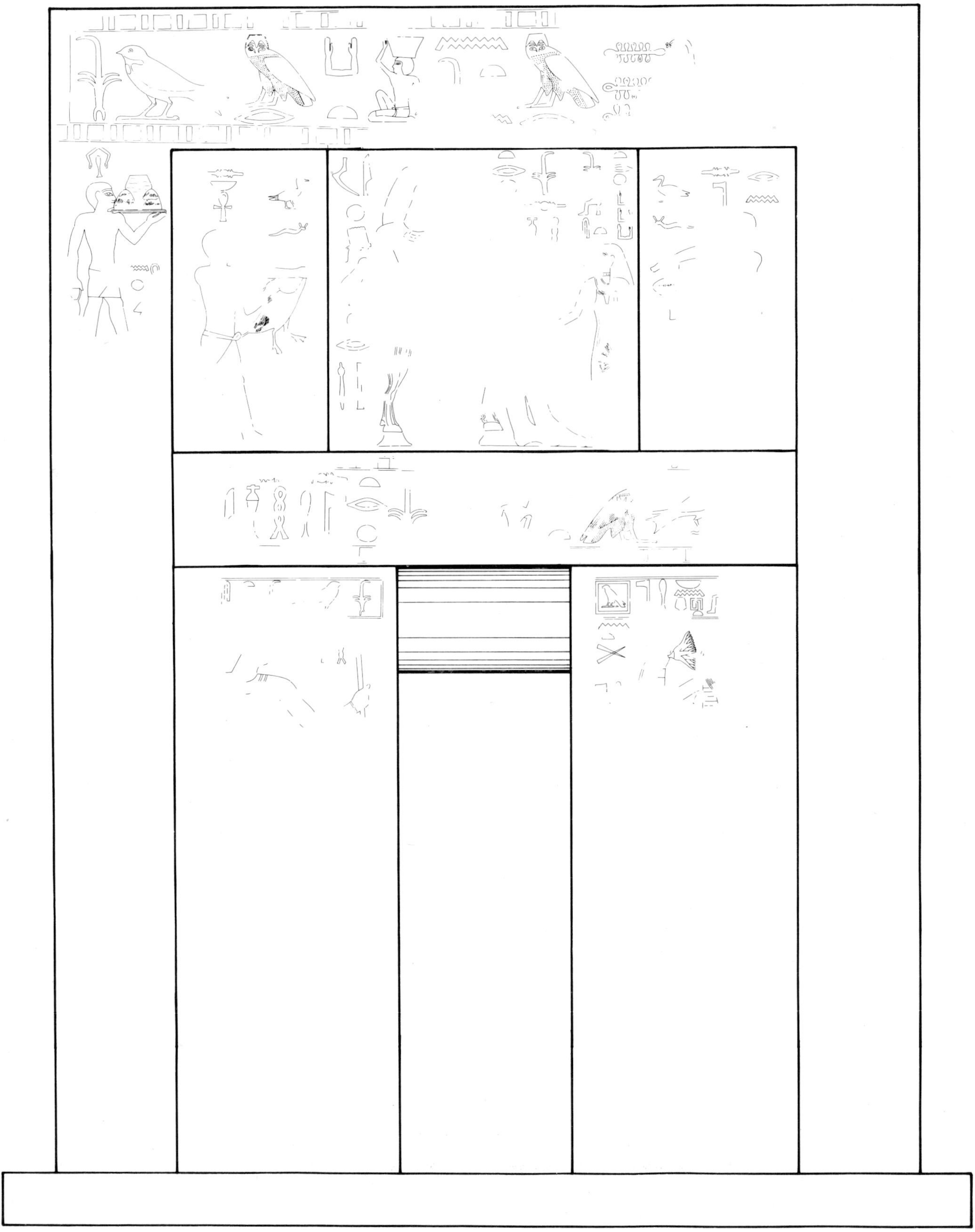

Fig. 15. Hesi-Min, shrine, west wall, false door

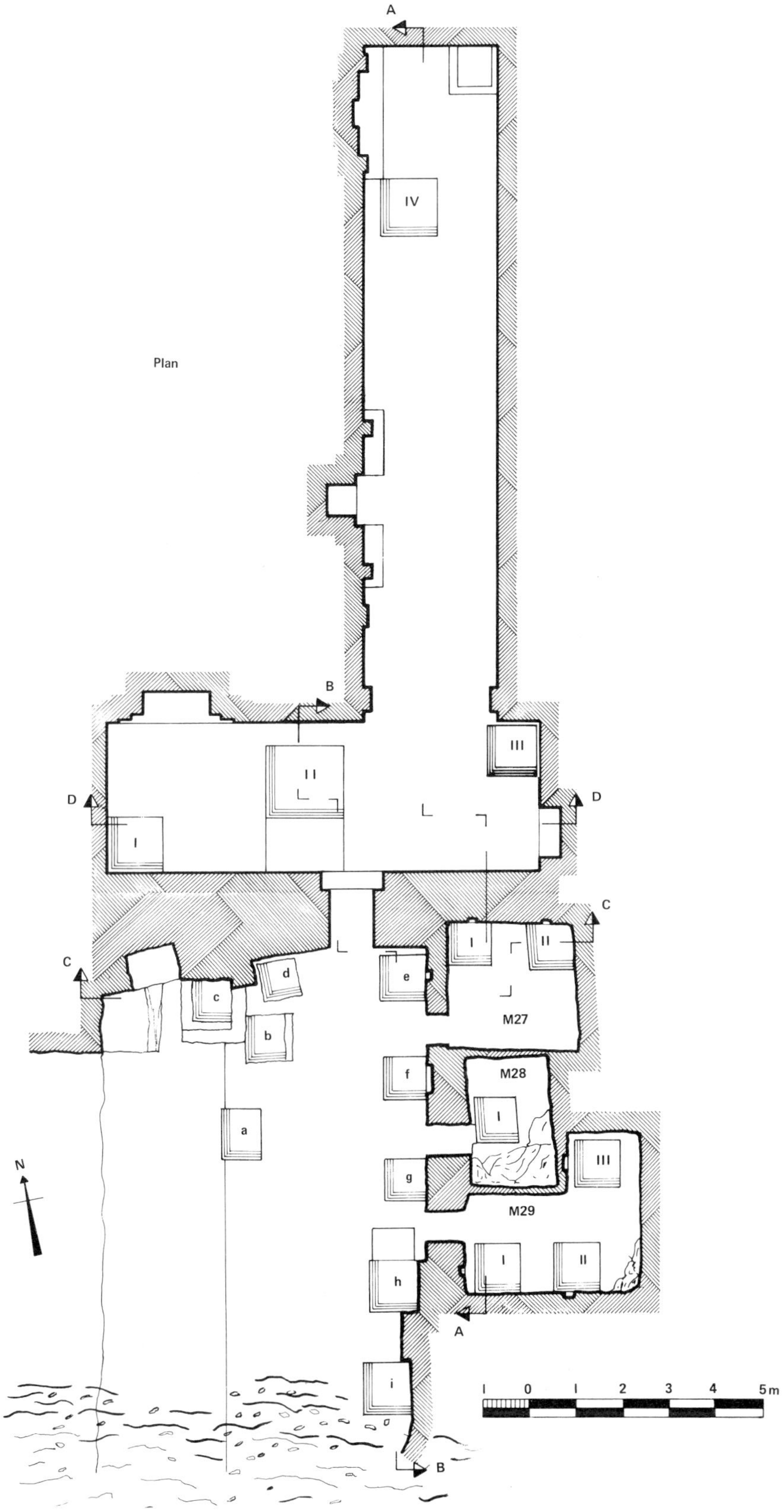

Fig. 1. Hesi-Min, plan

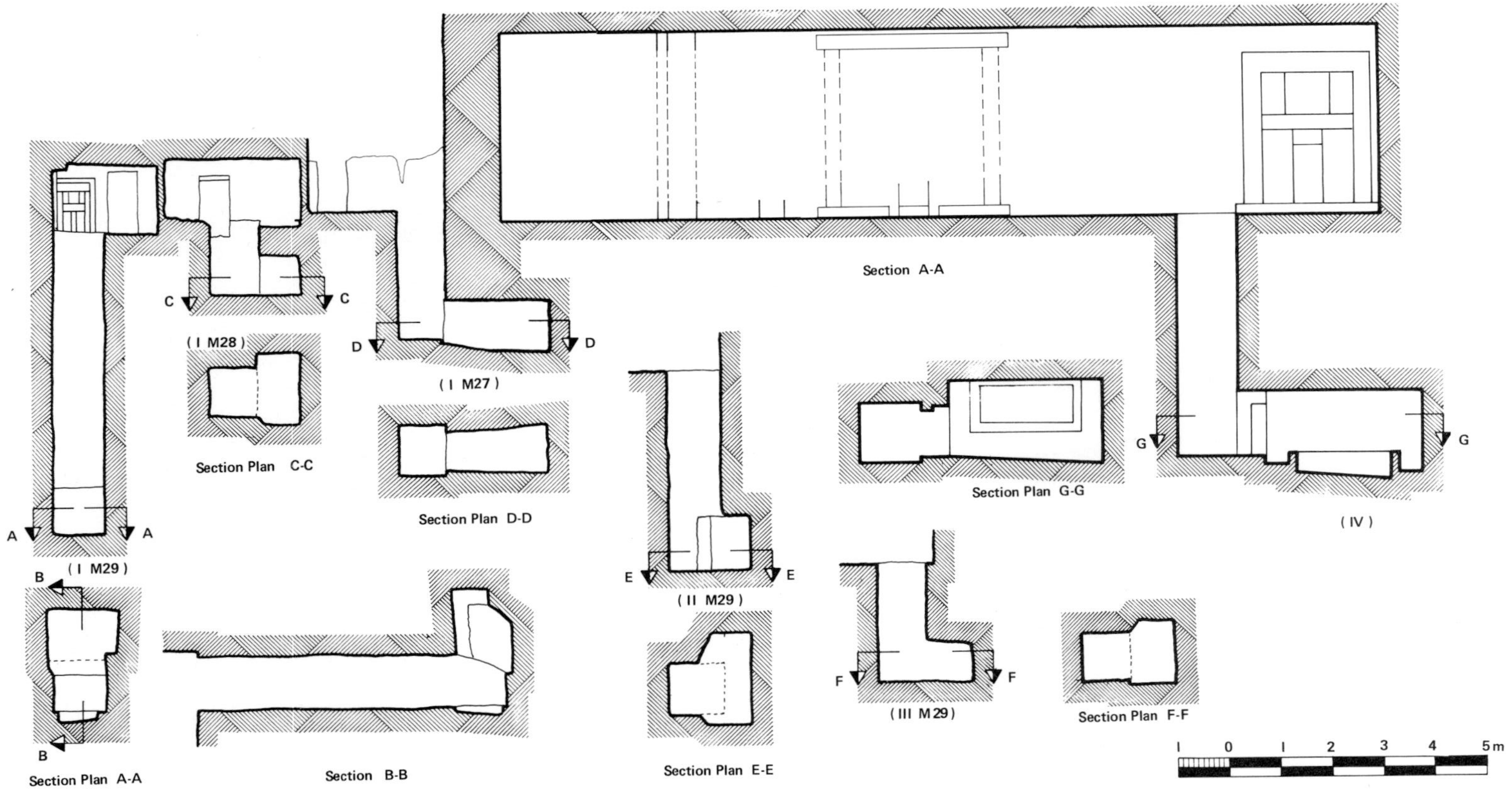

Fig. 2. Hesi-Min, section A-A

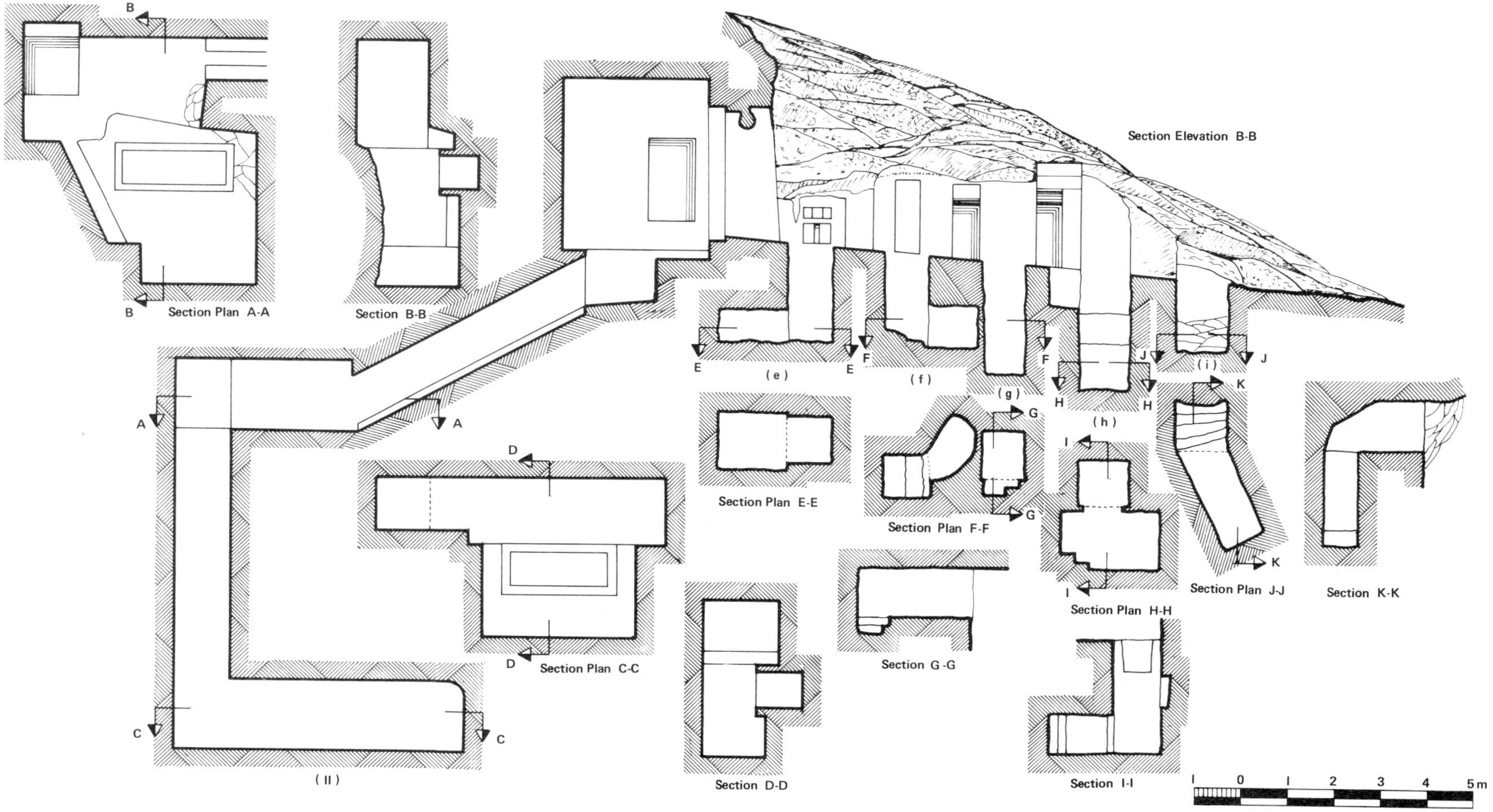

Fig. 3. Hesi-Min, section elevation B-B

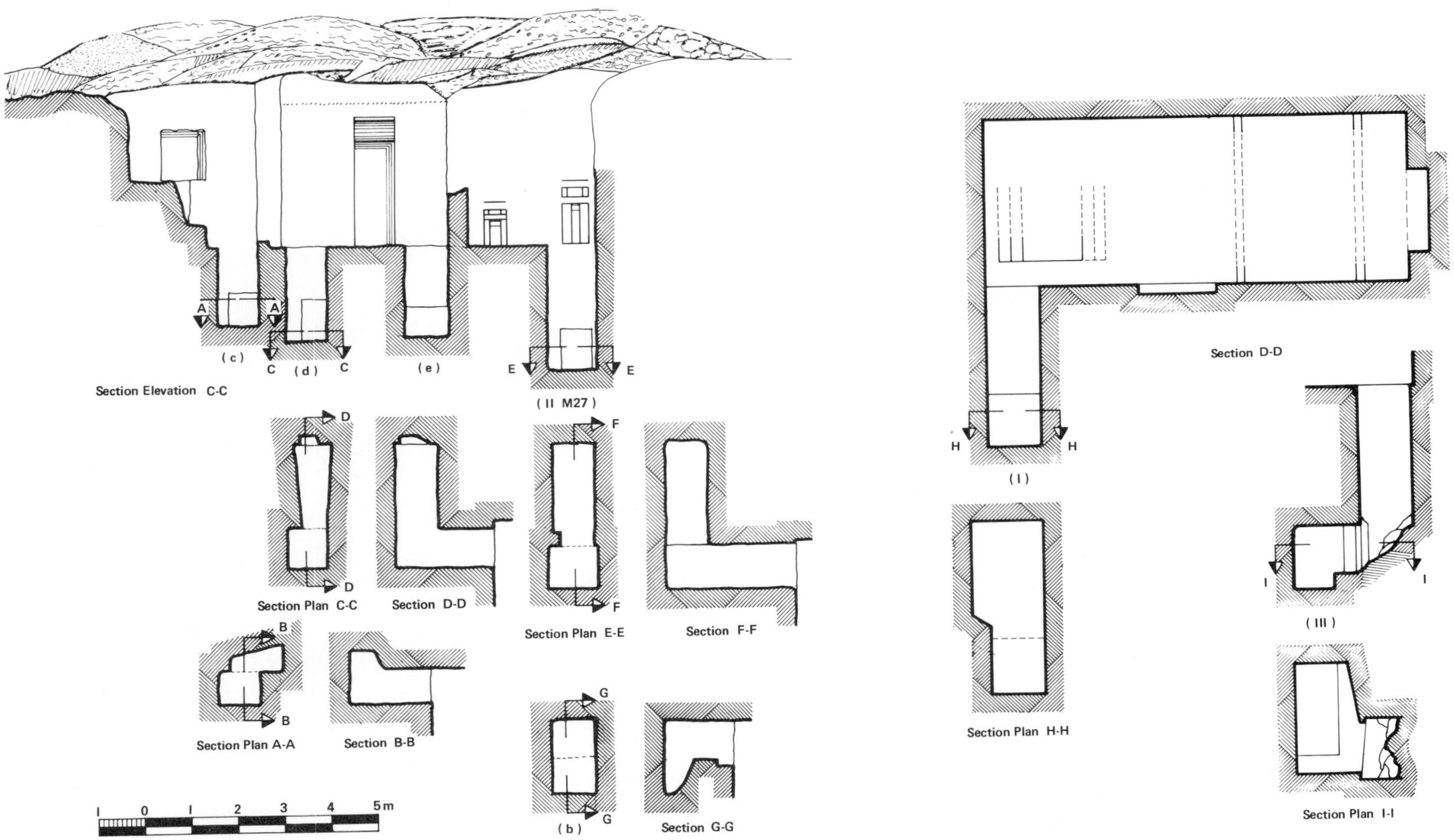

Fig. 4. Hesi-Min, section elevation C-C, section D-D

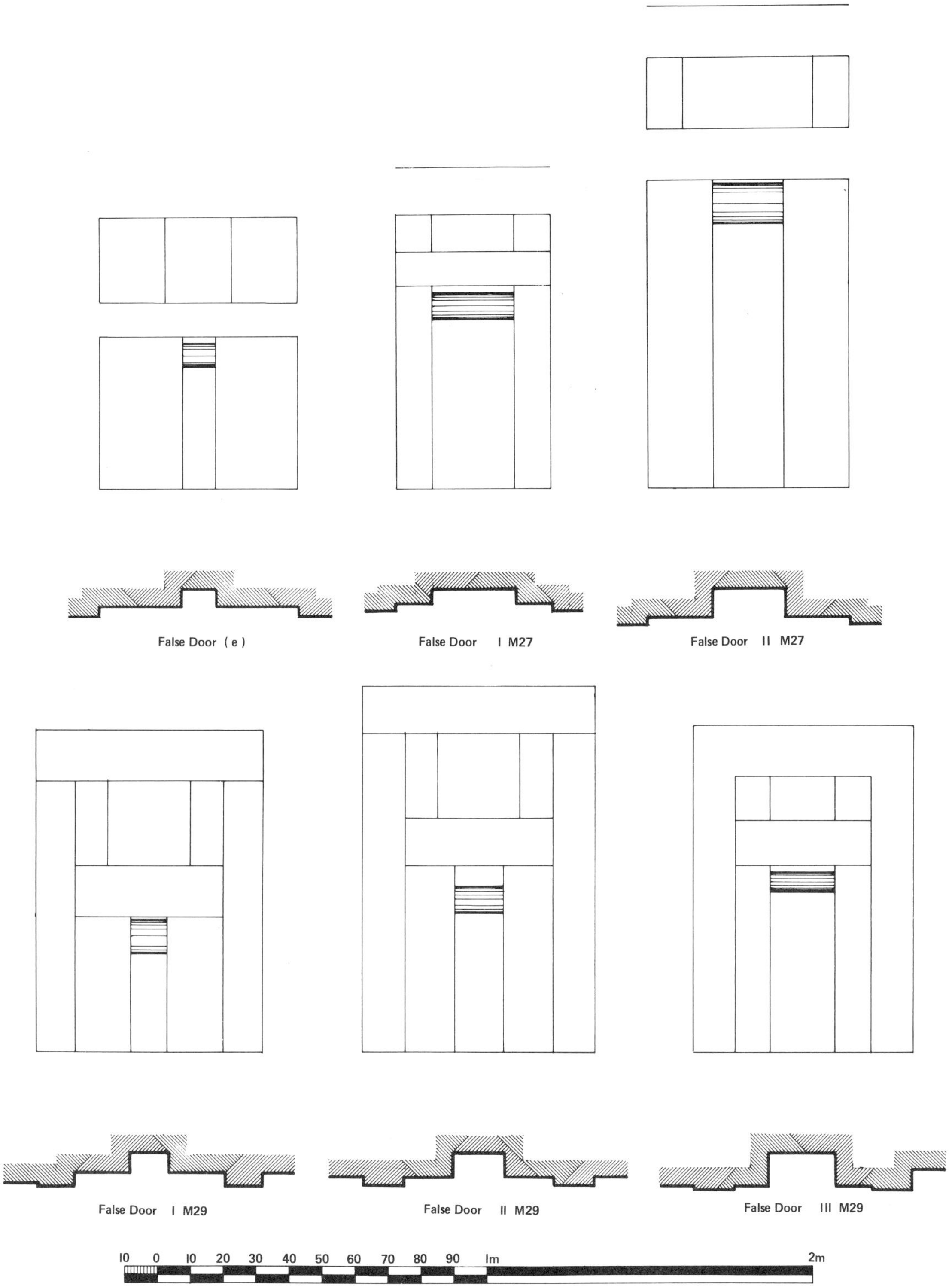

Fig. 5. False doors, tombs M22 (forecourt), M27, M29

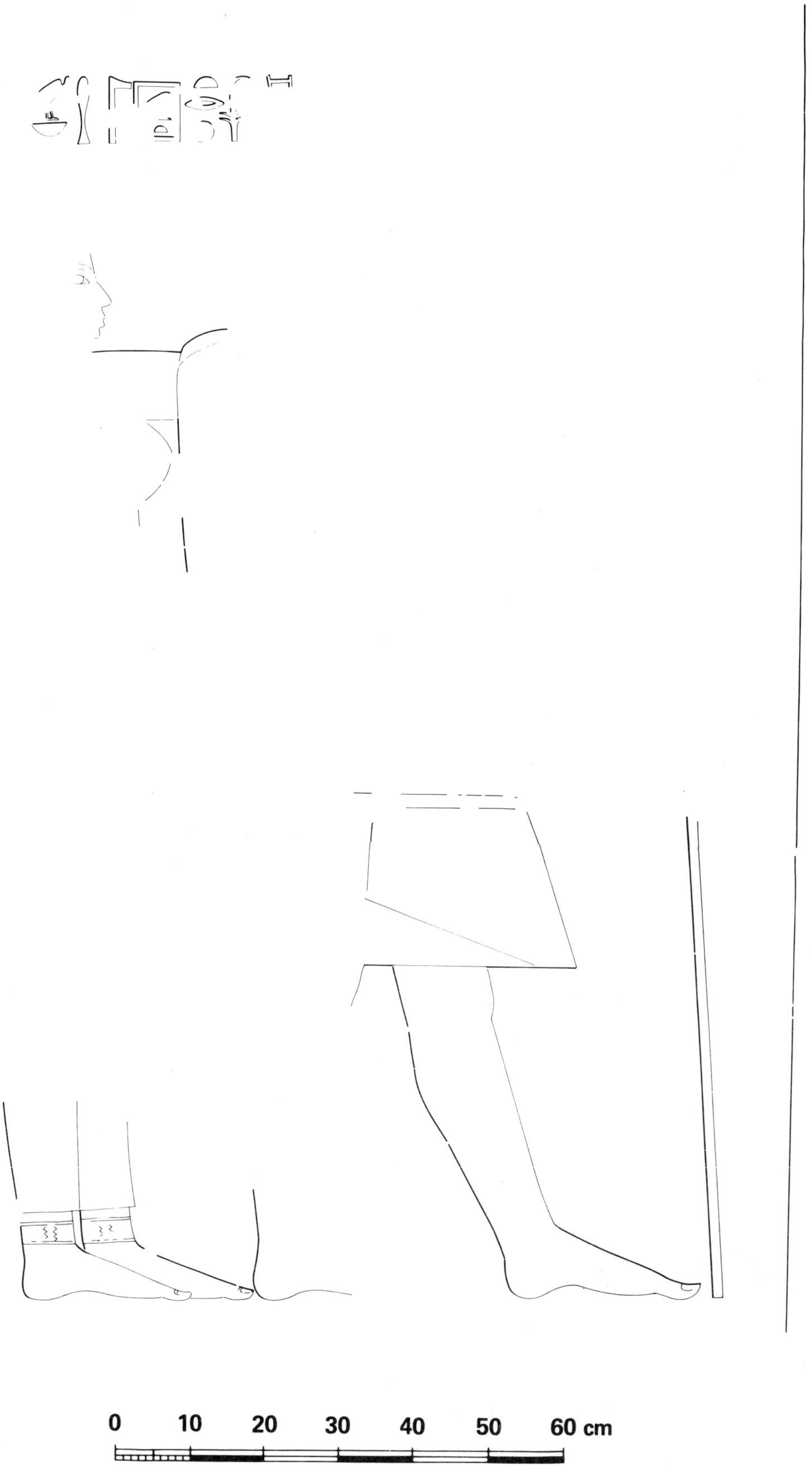

Fig. 6. Hesi-Min, entrance, right door thickness

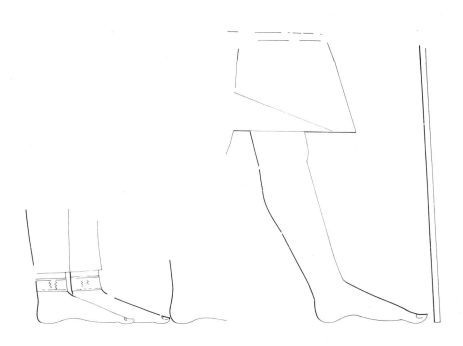

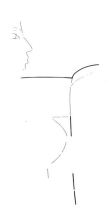

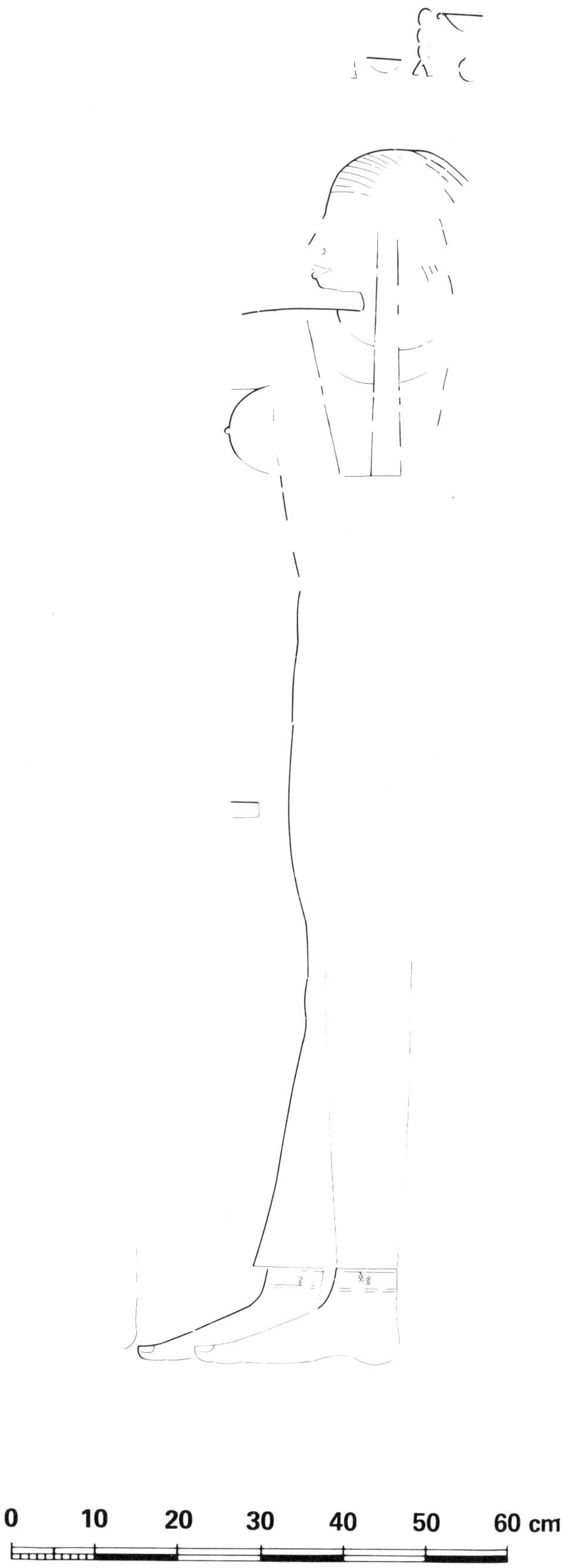

Fig. 7. Hesi-Min, entrance, left door thickness

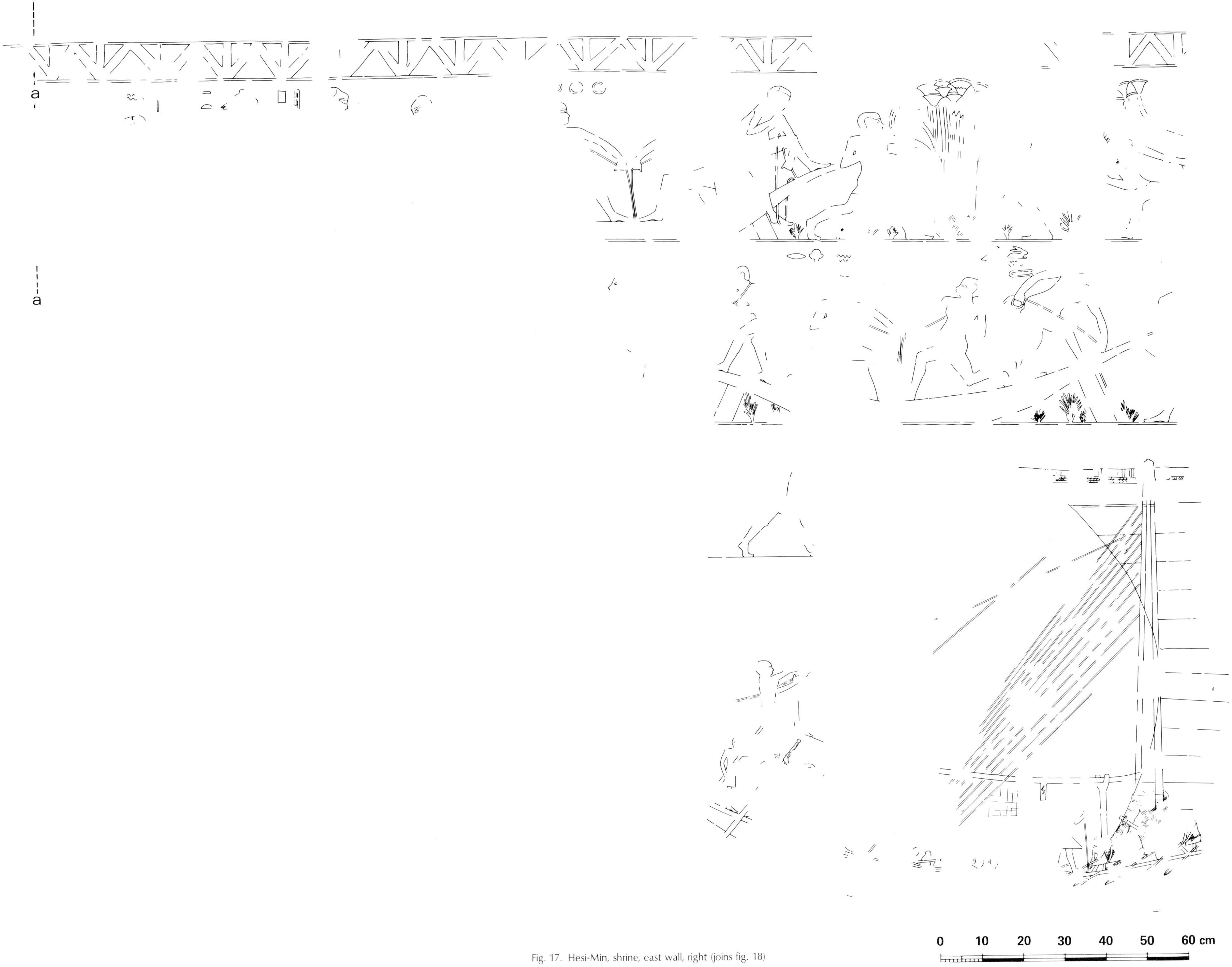

Fig. 17. Hesi-Min, shrine, east wall, right (joins fig. 18)

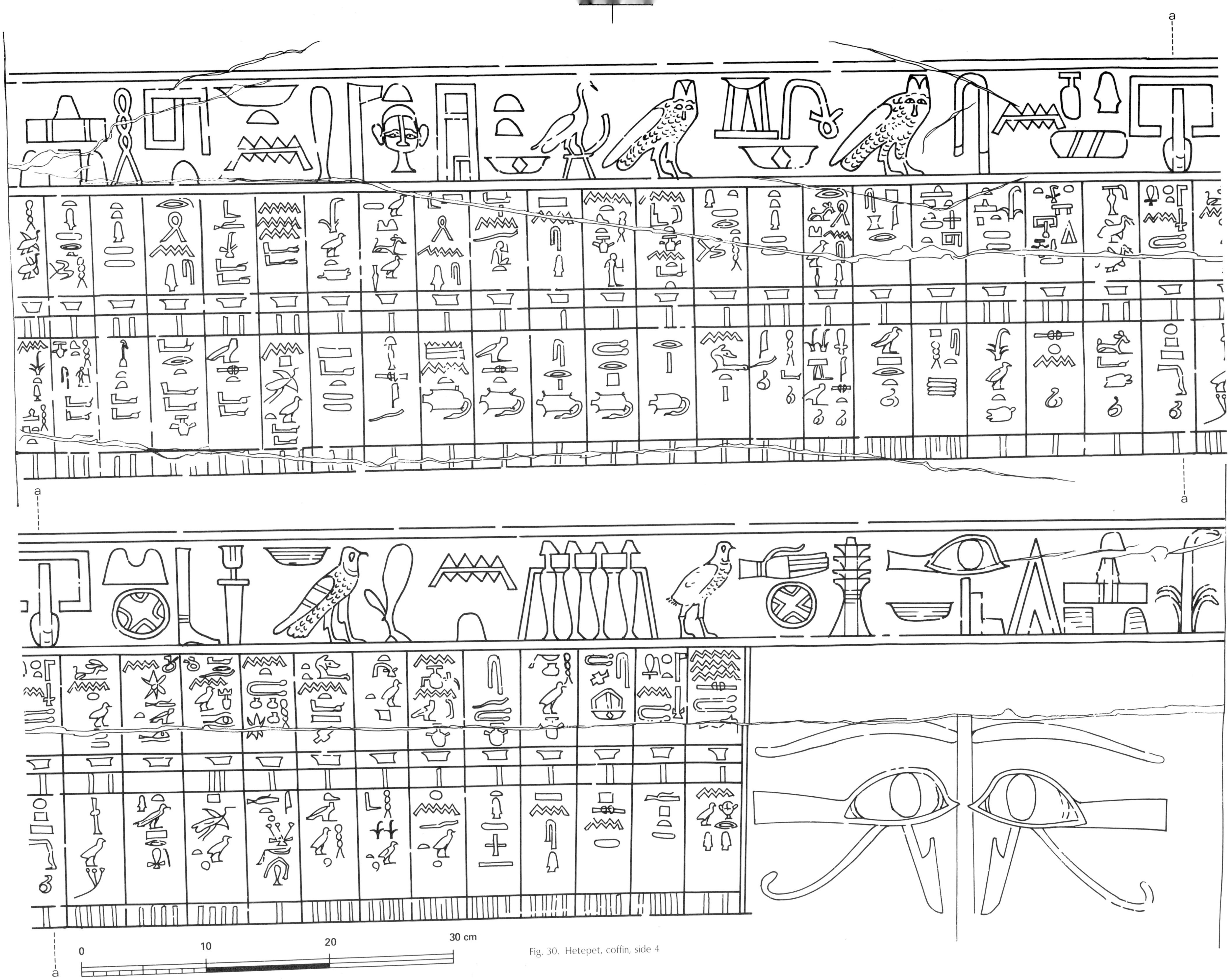

Fig. 30. Hetepet, coffin, side 4

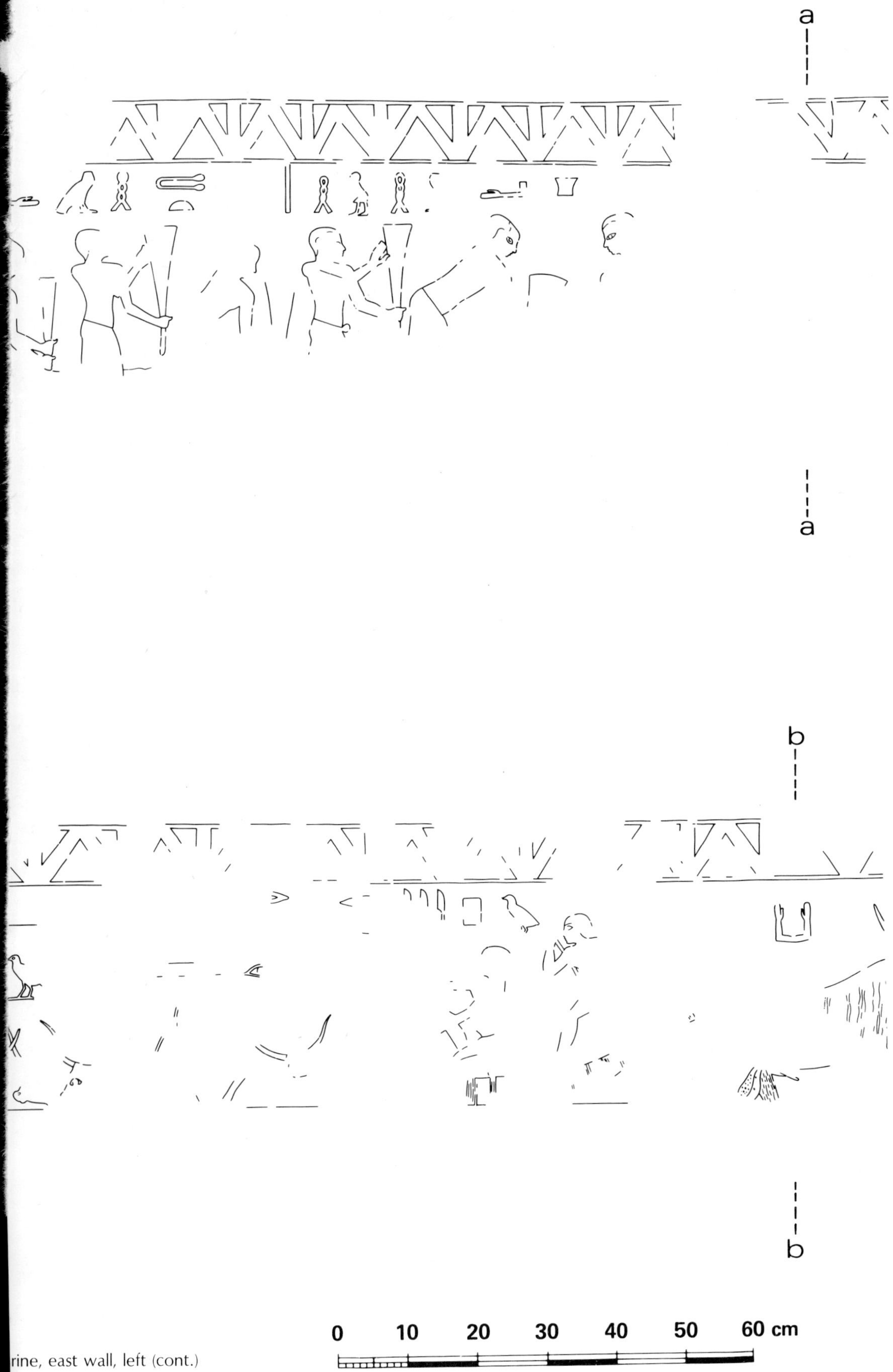

rine, east wall, left (cont.)

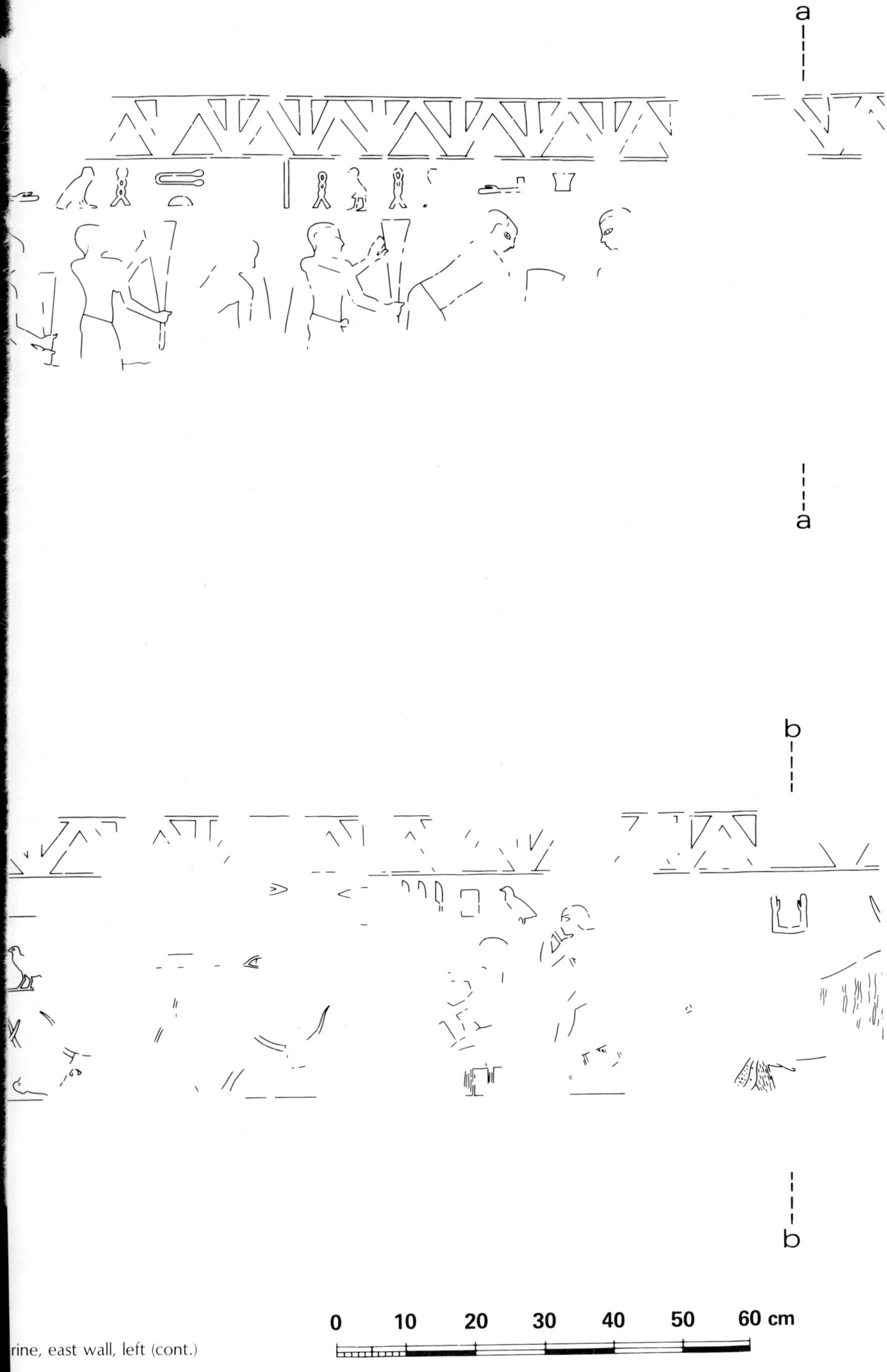

Fig. 18. Hesi-Min, s

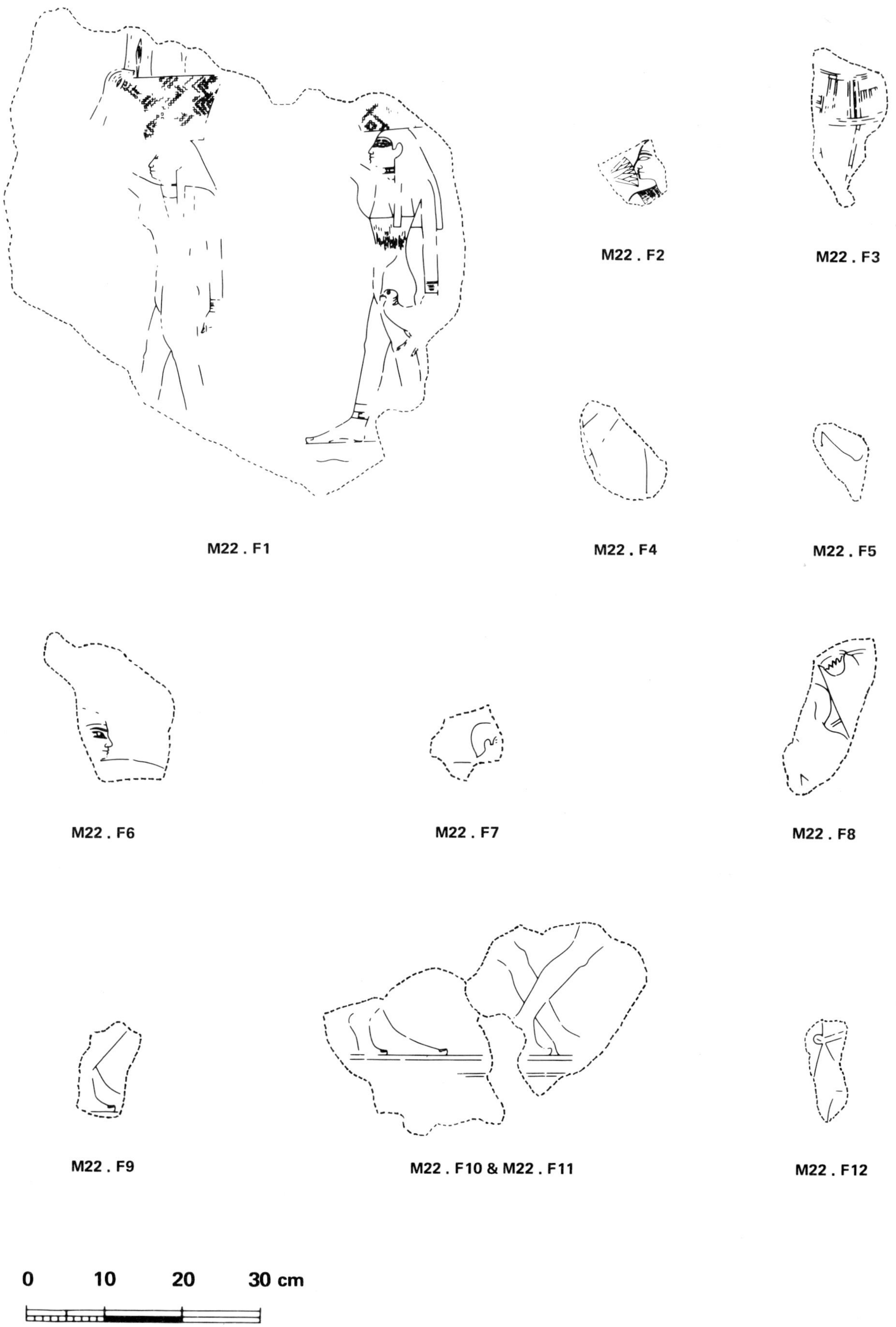

Fig. 19. Hesi-Min, decorated stone fragments

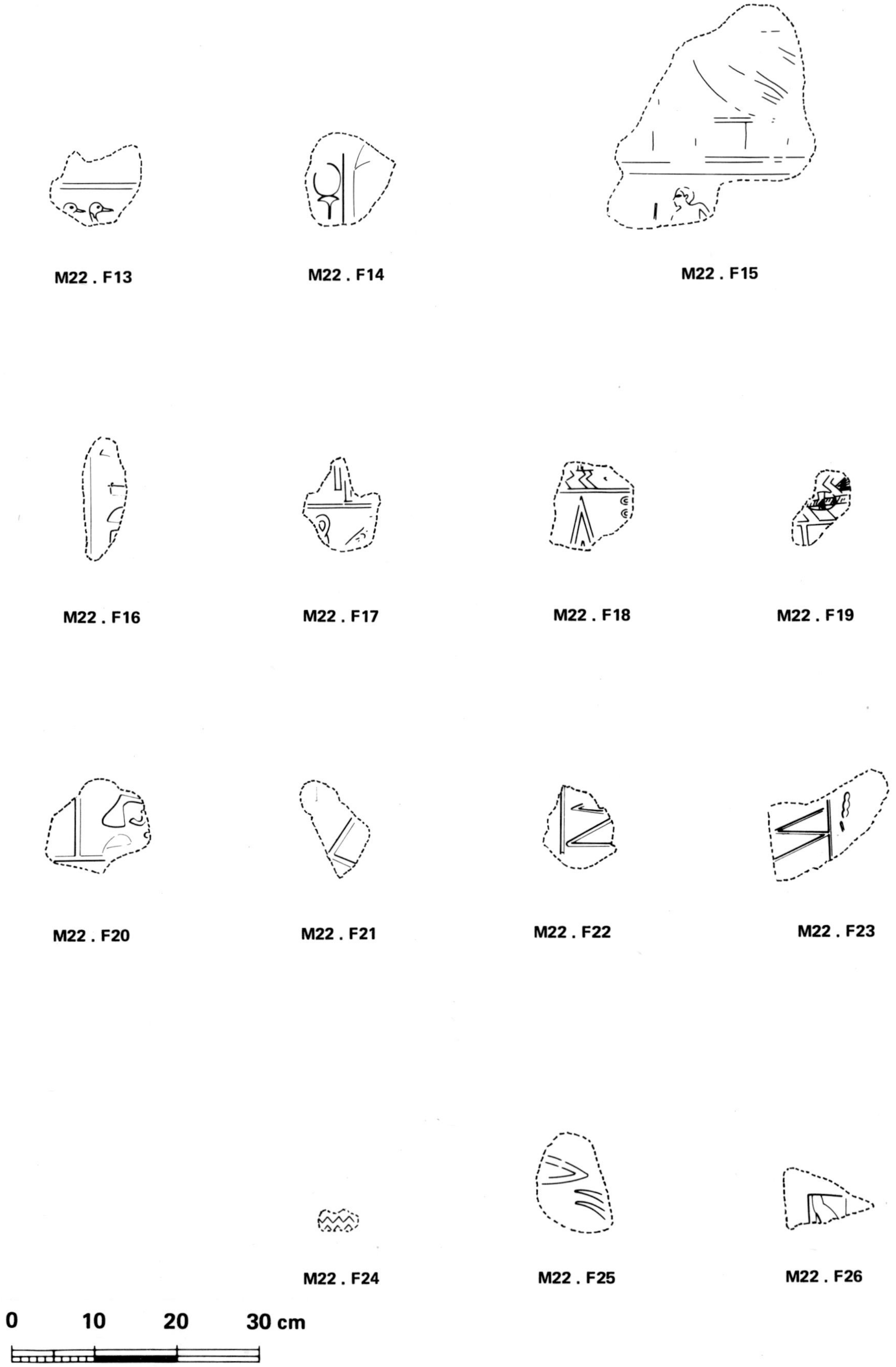

Fig. 20. Hesi-Min, decorated stone fragments

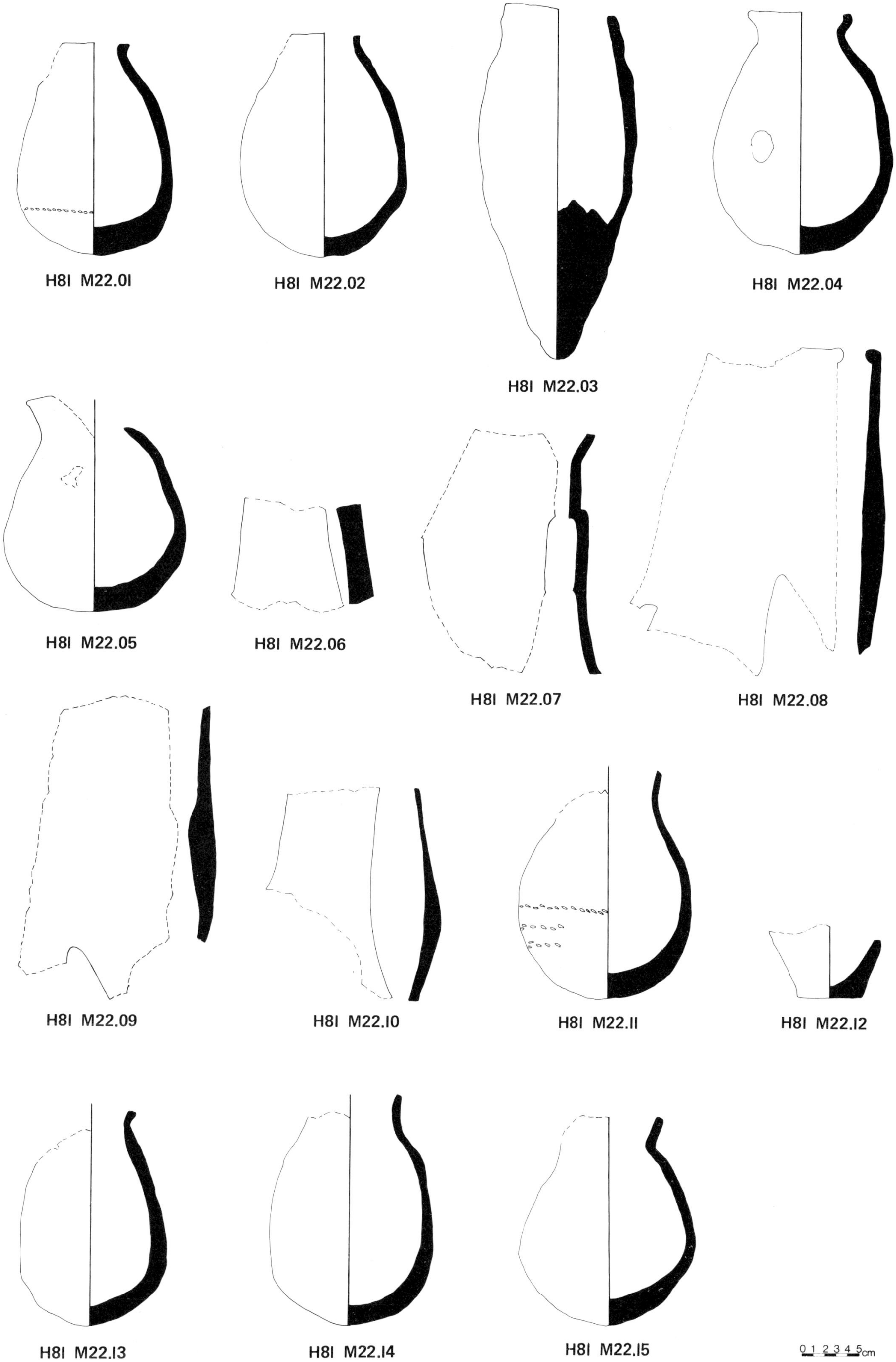

Fig. 21. Hesi-Min, pottery

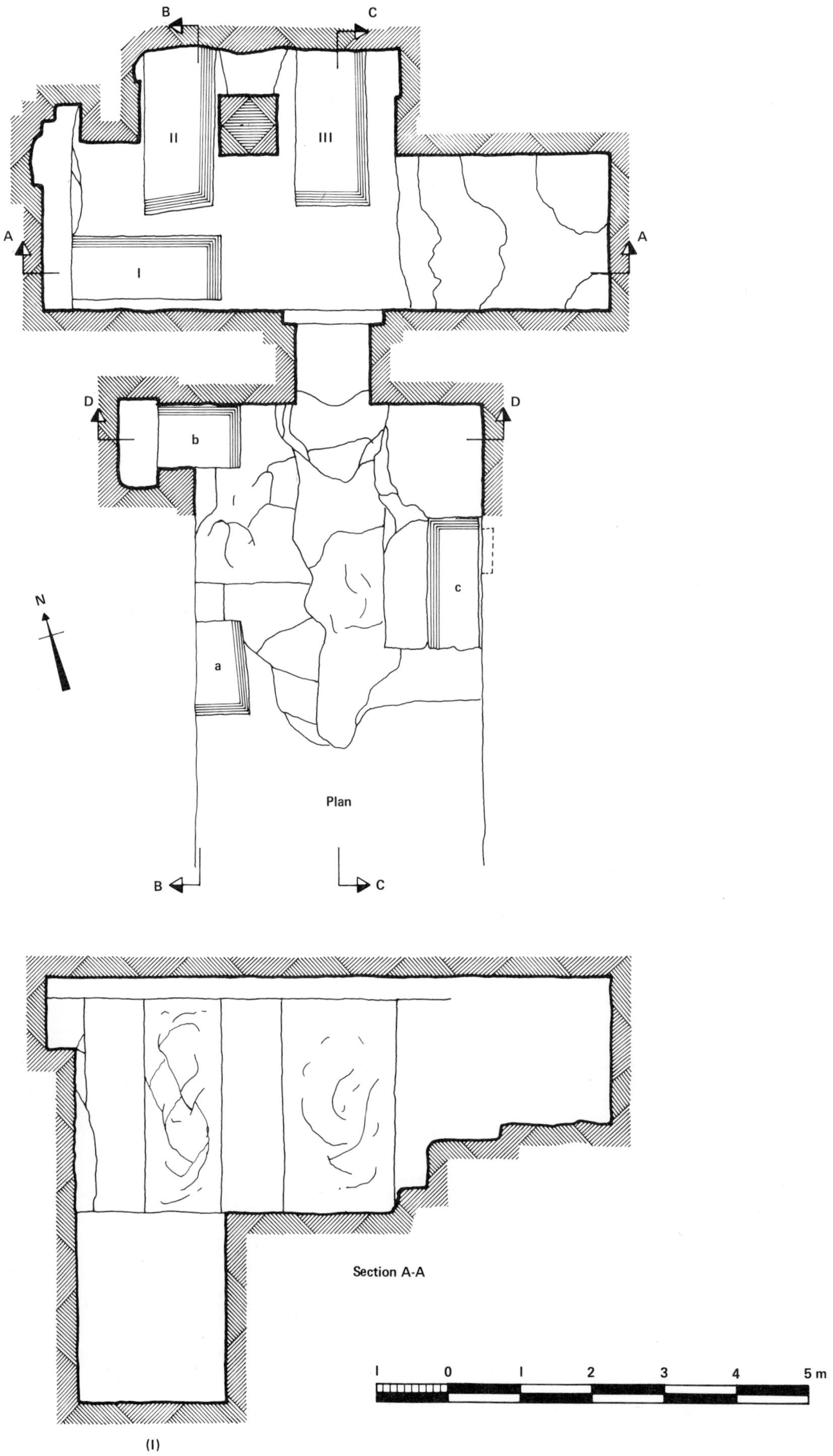

Fig. 22. Kheni-ankhu, plan, section A-A

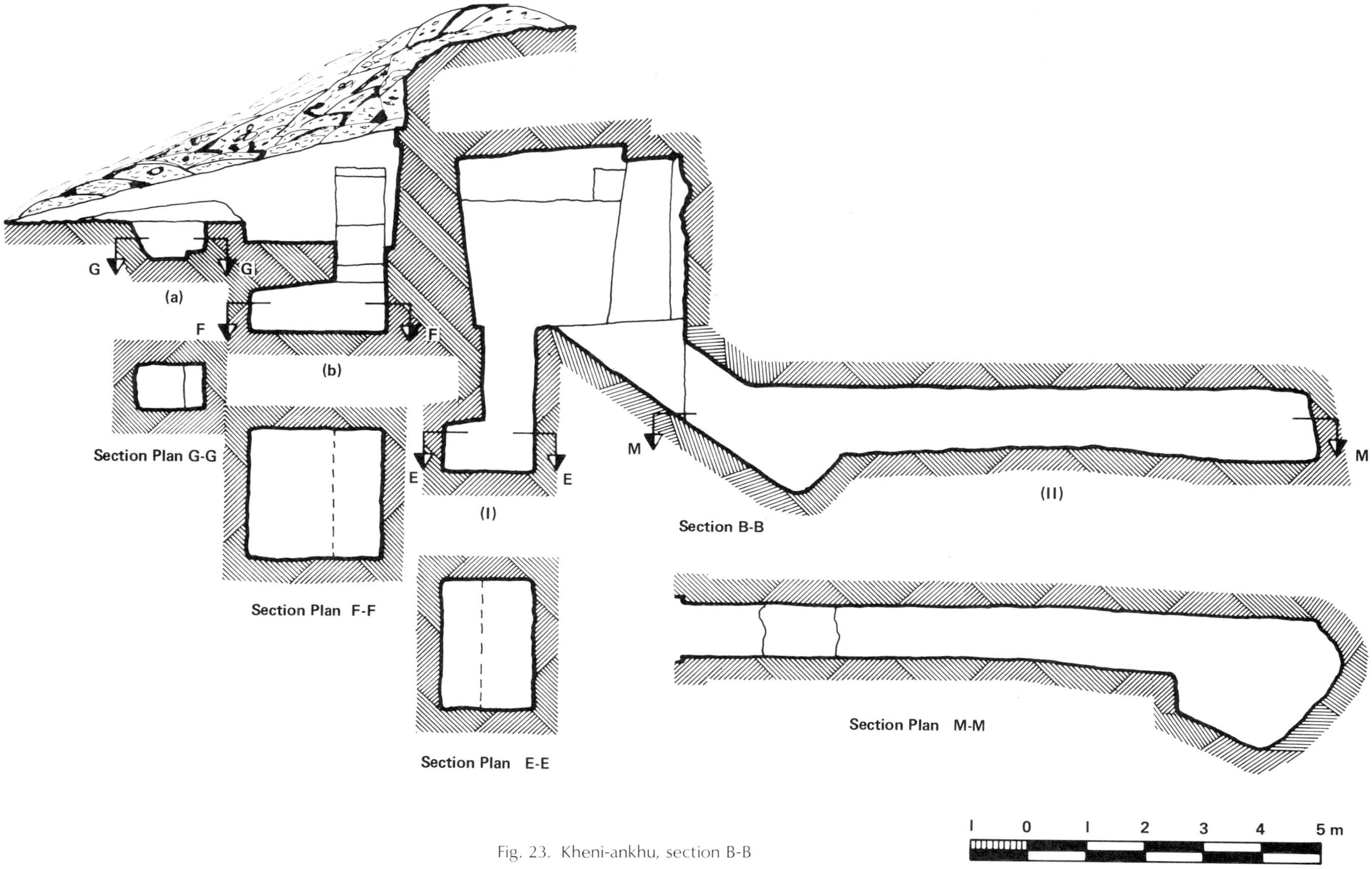

Fig. 23. Kheni-ankhu, section B-B

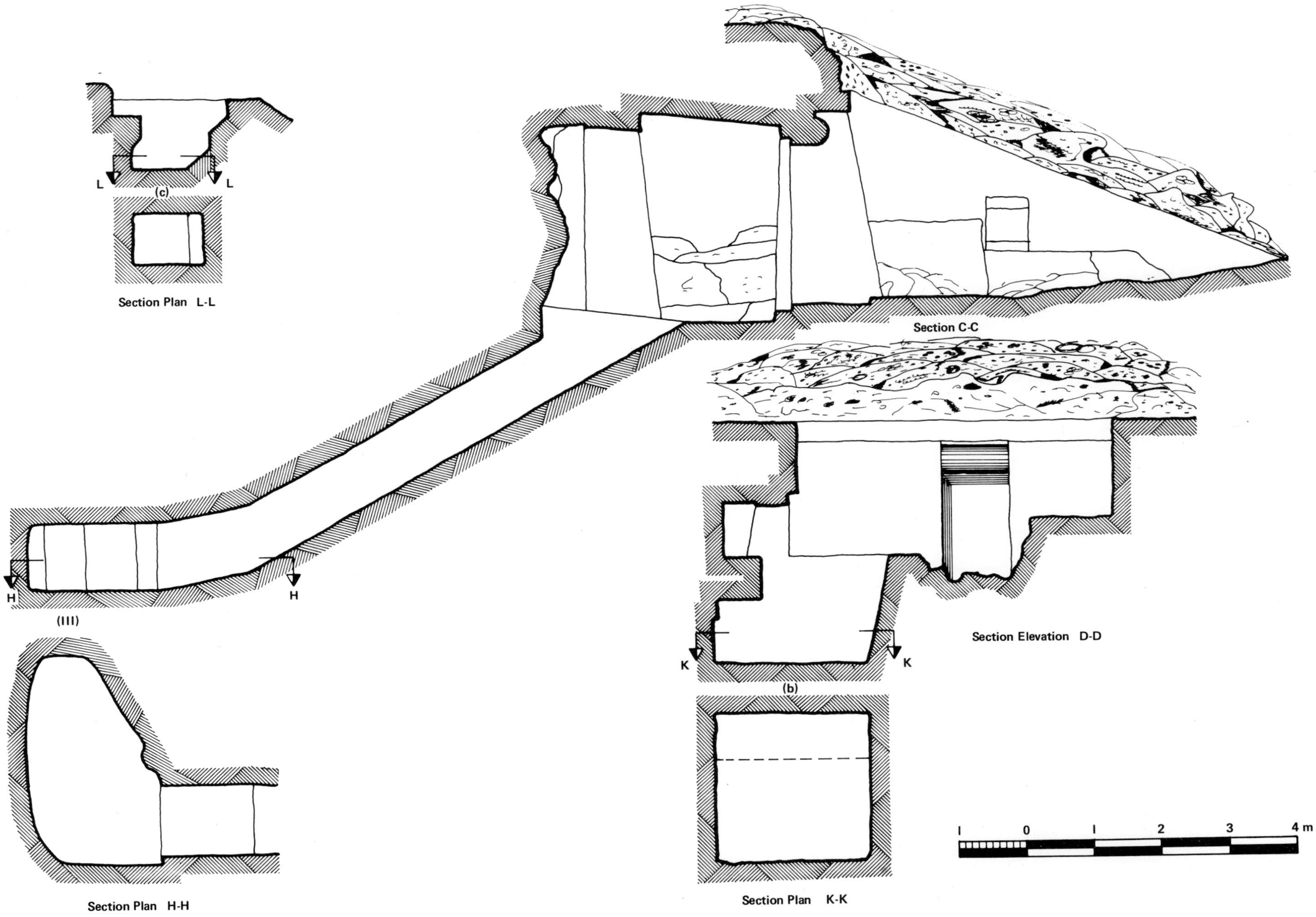

Fig. 24. Kheni-ankhu, section C-C, section elevation D-D

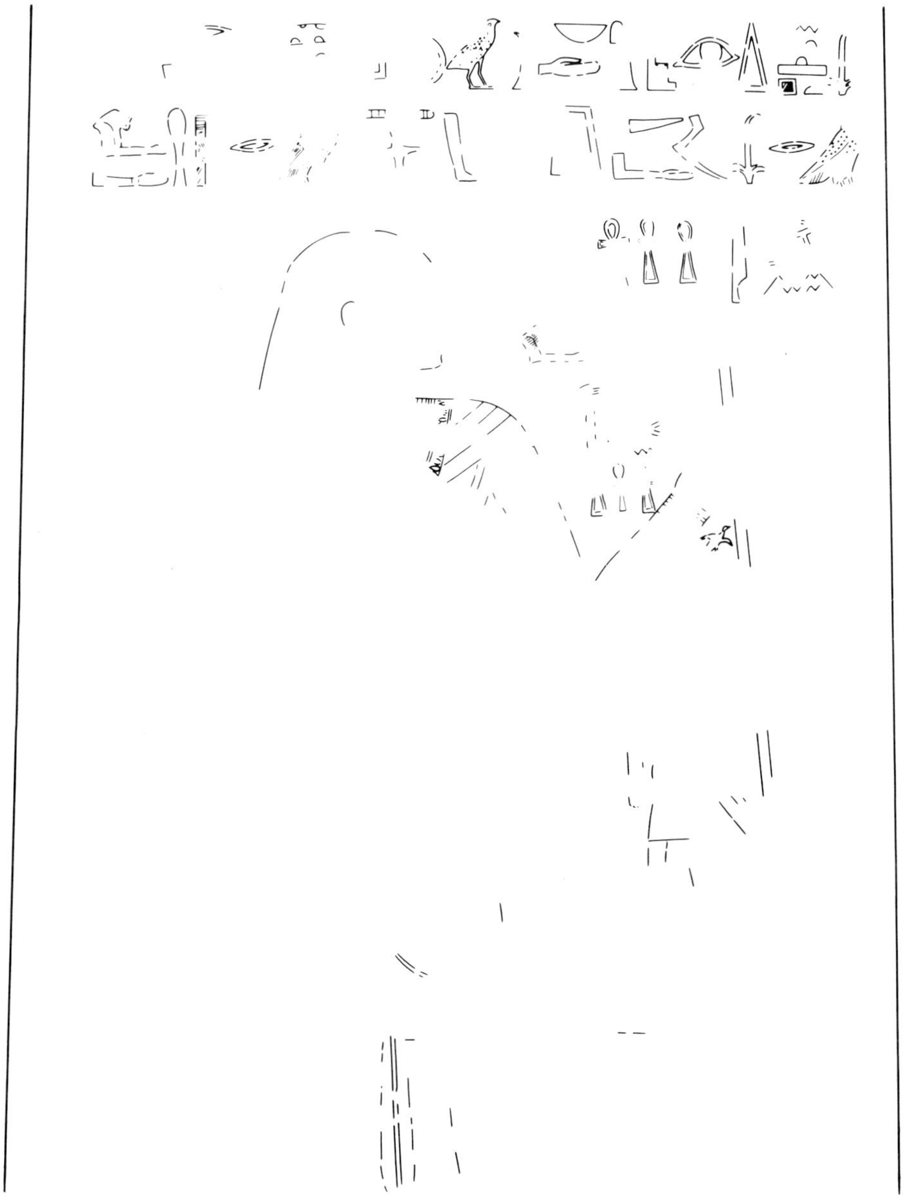

Fig. 25. Kheni-ankhu, chapel, south face of central pillar

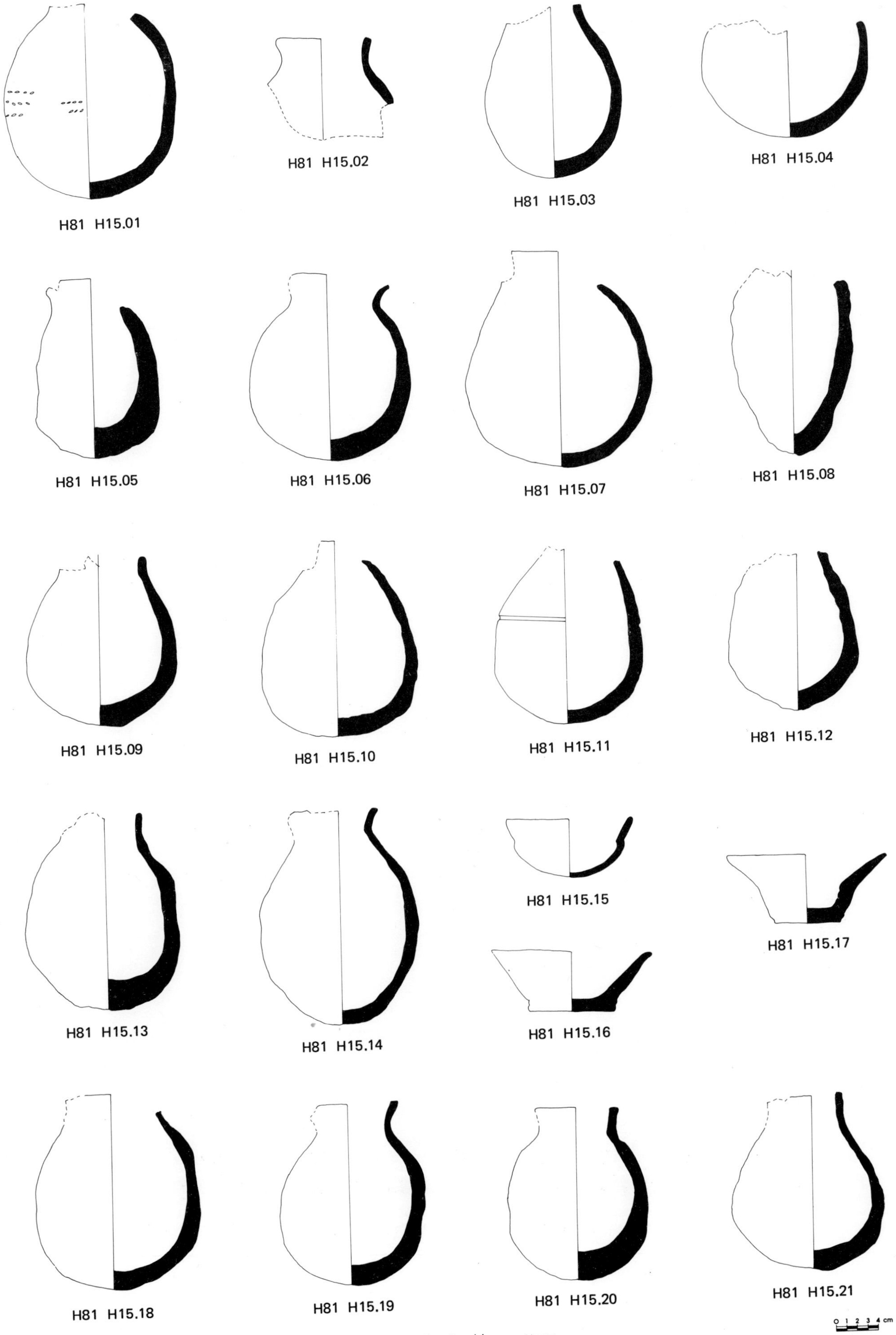

Fig. 26. Kheni-ankhu, pottery

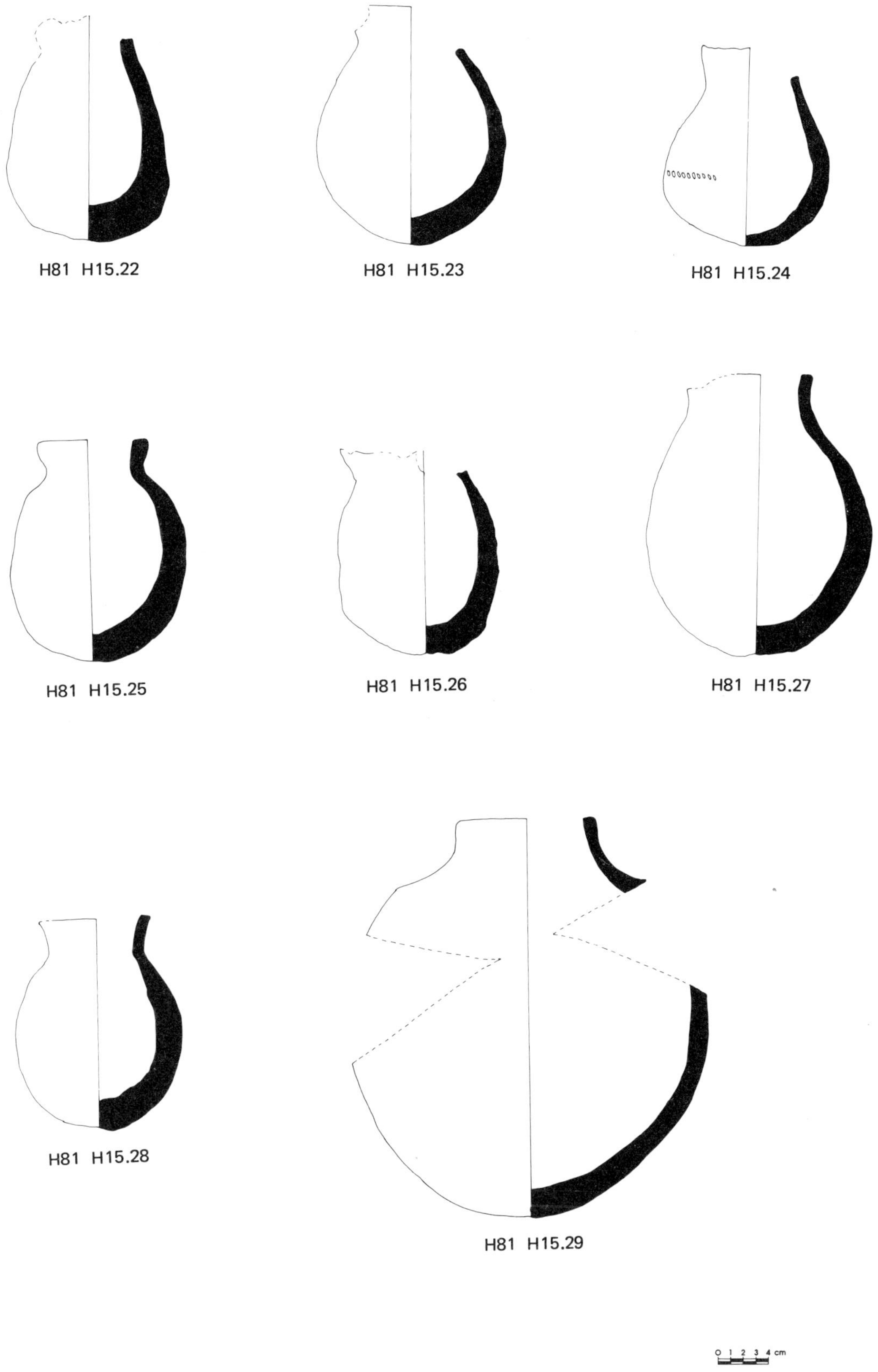

Fig. 27. Kheni-ankhu, pottery

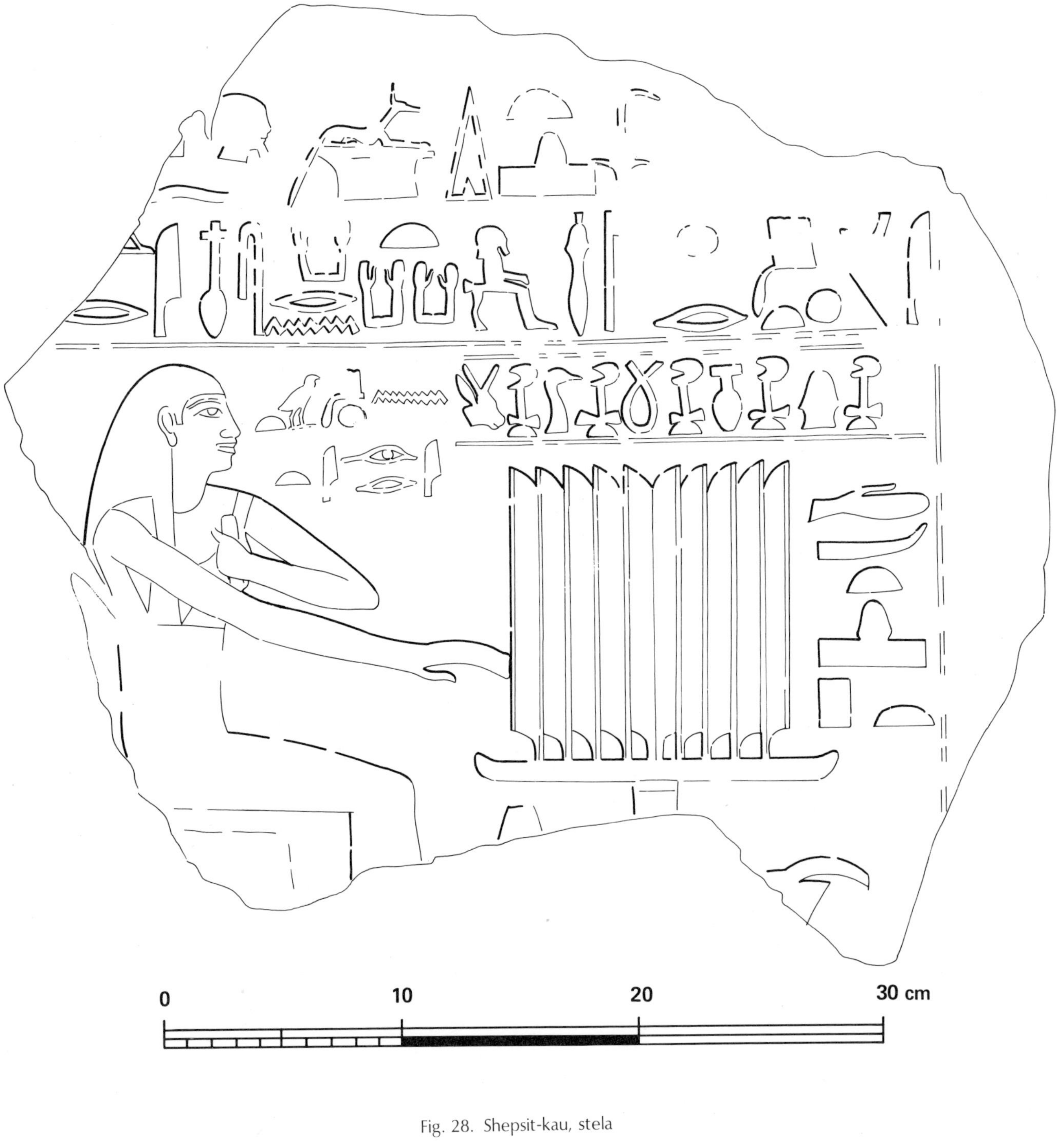

Fig. 28. Shepsit-kau, stela

(a) side 1

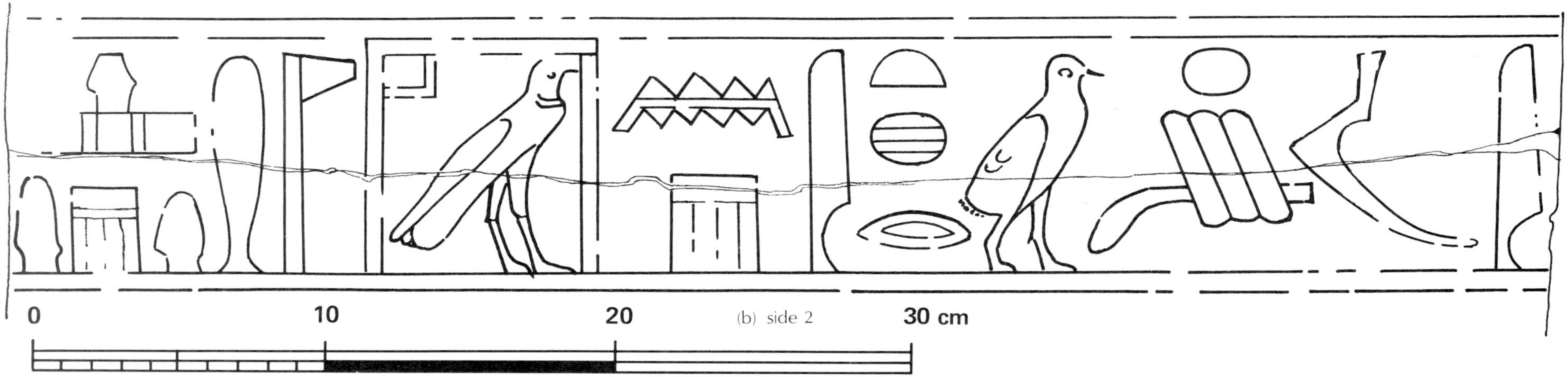

(b) side 2

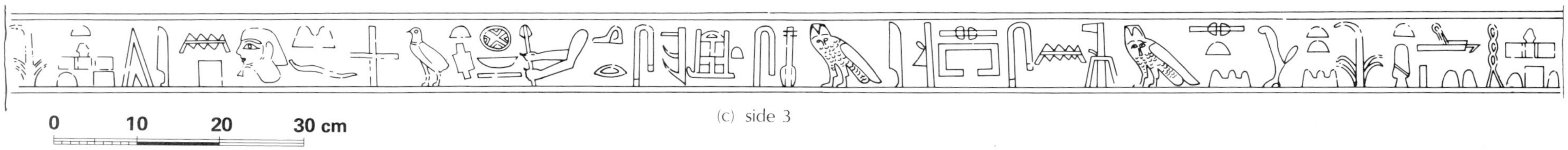

(c) side 3

Fig. 29. Hetepet, coffin

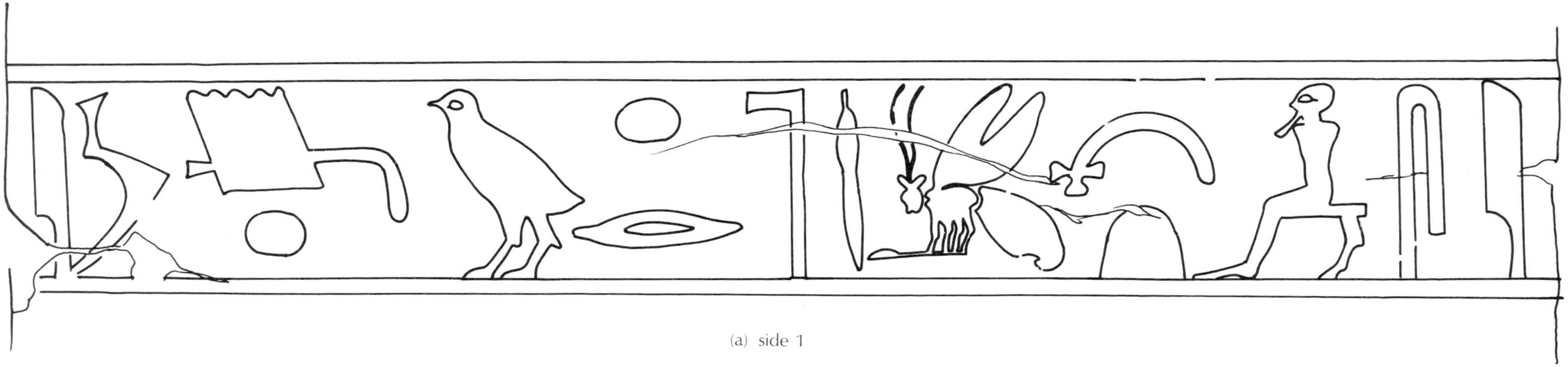

(a) side 1

(b) side 2

Fig. 31. Shepsi-pu-Min, coffin

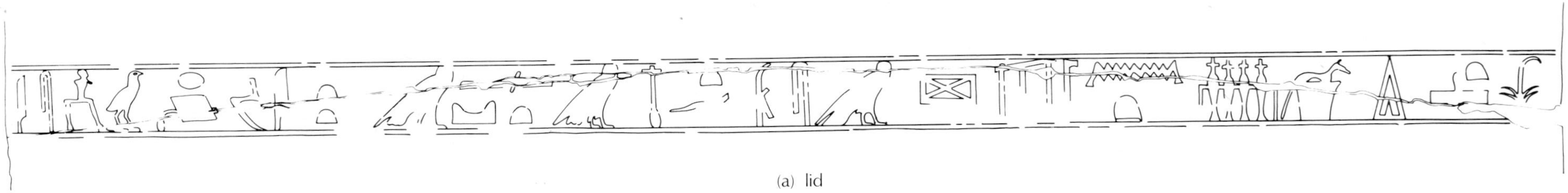
(a) lid

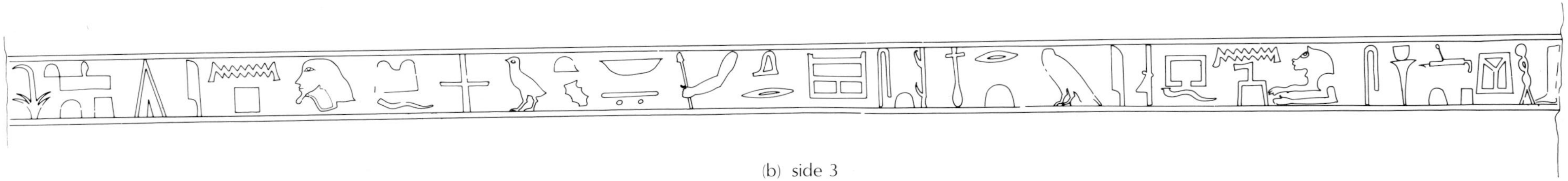
(b) side 3

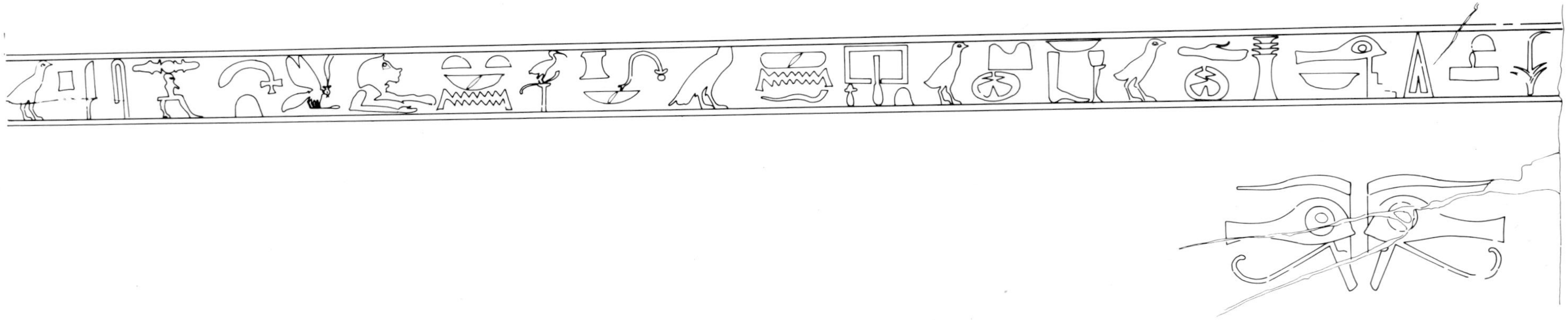
(c) side 4

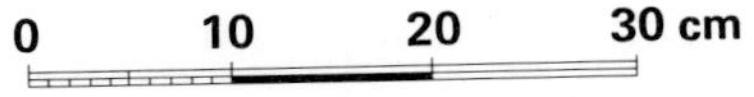

Fig. 32. Shepsi-pu-Min, coffin

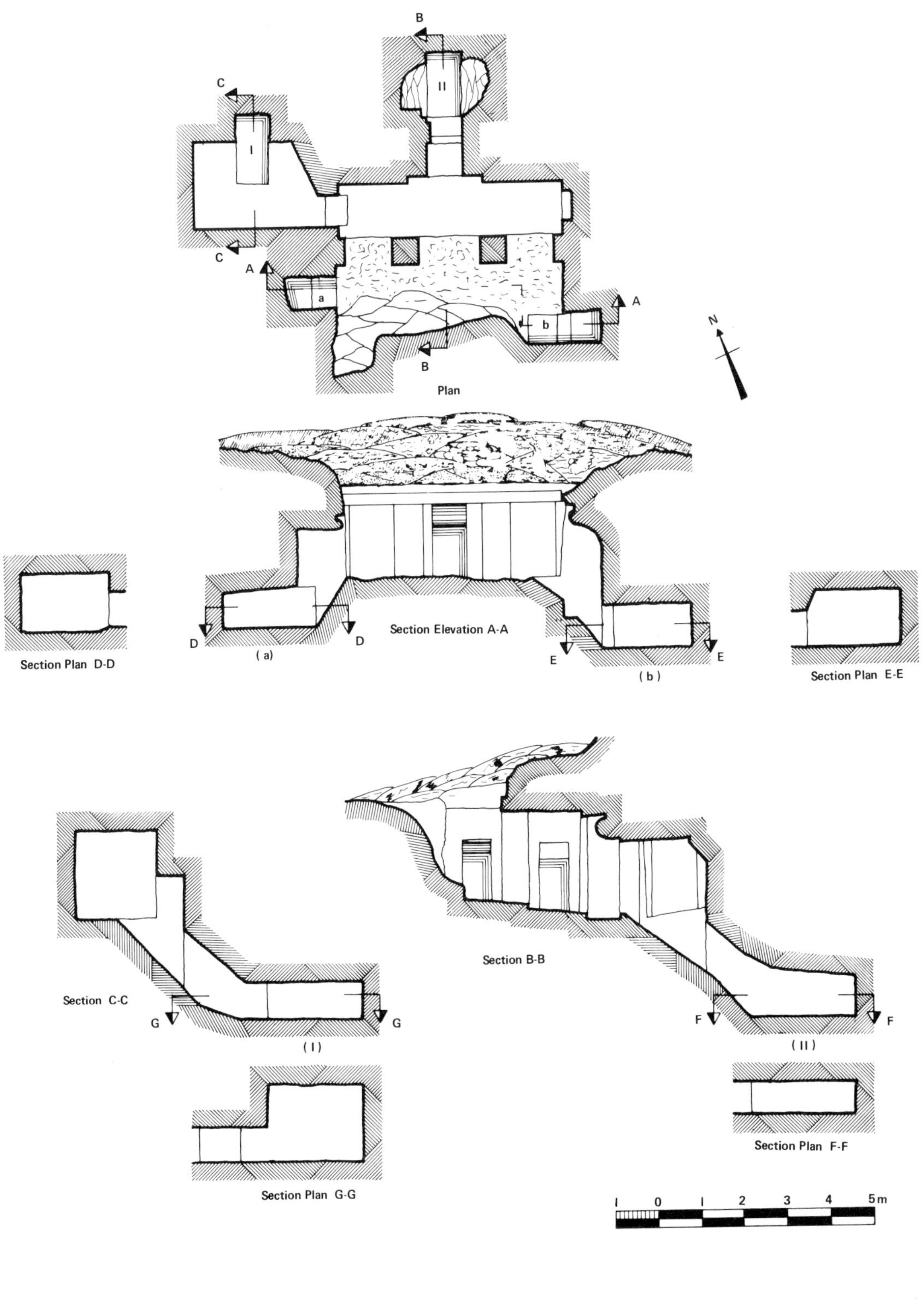

Fig. 33. H14, plan, section elevation A-A, section B-B, section C-C

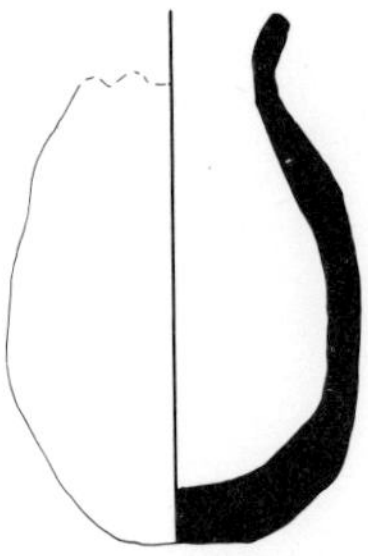

H82 H14.01

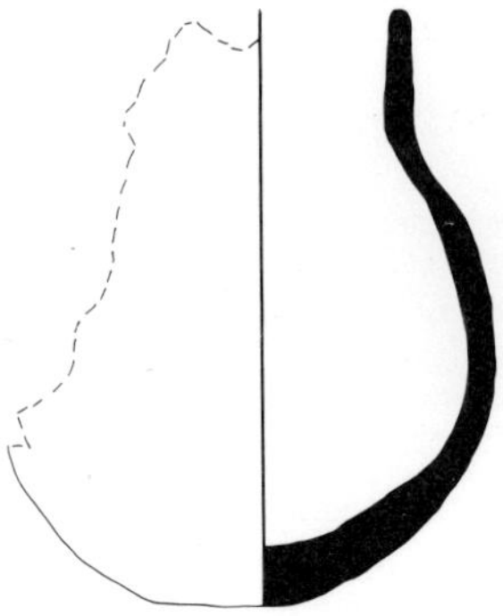

H82 H14.02

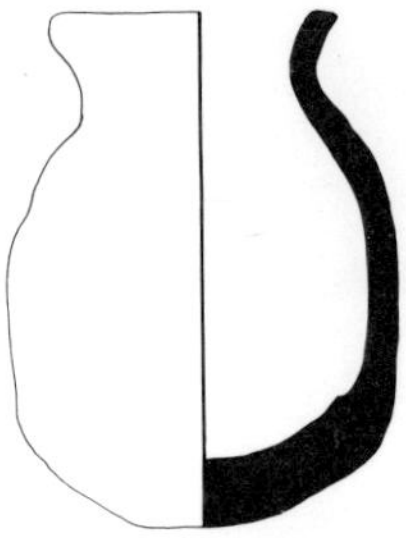

H82 H14.03

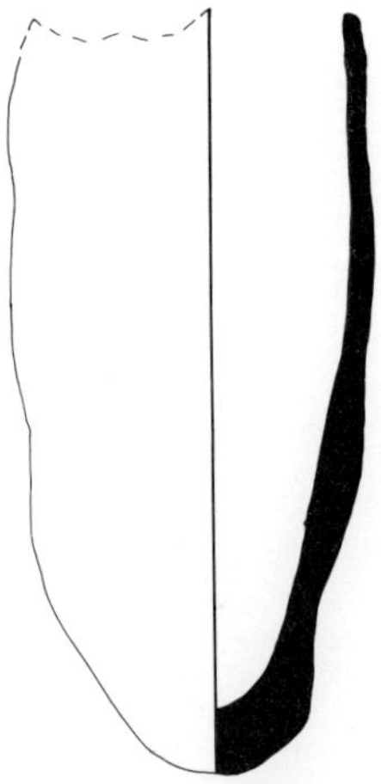

H82 H14.04

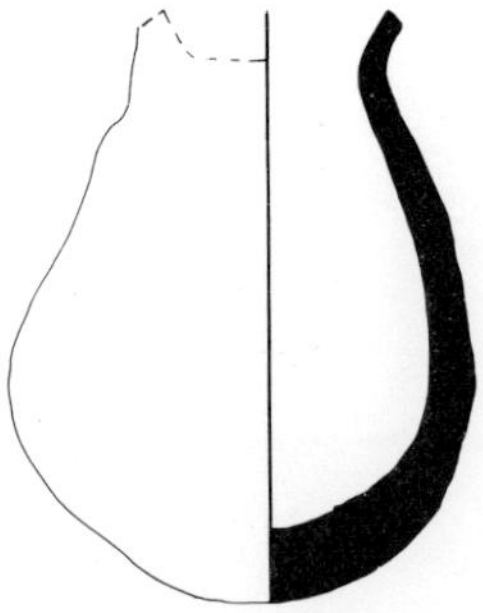

H82 H14.05

Fig. 34. H14, pottery